Endorsements for the Flourish Bible Study Series

"The brilliant and beautiful mix of sound teaching, helpful charts, lists, sidebars, and appealing graphics—as well as insightful questions that get the reader into the text of Scripture—make these studies that women will want to invest time in and will look back on as time well spent."

Nancy Guthrie, Bible teacher; author, *Even Better than Eden*

"My daughter and I love using Flourish Bible Studies for our morning devotions. Lydia Brownback's faithful probing of biblical texts; insightful questions; invitations to engage in personal applications using additional biblical texts and historical contexts; and commitment to upholding the whole counsel of God as it bears on living life as a godly woman has drawn us closer to the Lord and to his word. Brownback never sidesteps hard questions or hard providences, but neither does she appeal to discourses of victimhood or therapy, which are painfully common in the genre of women's Bible studies. I cannot recommend this series highly enough. My daughter and I look forward to working through this whole series together!"

Rosaria Butterfield, Former Professor of English, Syracuse University; author, *The Gospel Comes with a House Key*

"As a women's ministry leader, I am excited about the development of the Flourish Bible Study series, which will not only prayerfully equip women to increase in biblical literacy but also come alongside them to build a systematic and comprehensive framework to become lifelong students of the word of God. This series provides visually engaging studies with accessible content that will not only strengthen the believer but the church as well."

Karen Hodge, Coordinator of Women's Ministries, Presbyterian Church in America; coauthor, *Transformed*

"Lydia Brownback is an experienced Bible teacher who has dedicated her life to ministry roles that help women (and men) grow in Christ. With a wealth of biblical, historical, and theological content, her Flourish Bible Studies are ideal for groups and individuals that are serious about the in-depth study of the word of God."

Phil and Lisa Ryken, President, Wheaton College; and his wife, Lisa

"If you're looking for rich, accessible, and deeply biblical Bible studies, this series is for you! Lydia Brownback leads her readers through different books of the Bible, providing background information, maps, timelines, and questions that probe the text in order to glean understanding and application. She settles us deeply in the context of a book as she highlights God's unfolding plan of redemption and rescue. You will learn, you will delight in God's word, and you will love our good King Jesus even more."

Courtney Doctor, Coordinator of Women's Initiatives, The Gospel Coalition; author, *From Garden to Glory* and *Steadfast*

"Lydia Brownback's Bible study series provides a faithful guide to book after book. You'll find rich insights into context and good questions to help you study and interpret the Bible. Page by page, the studies point you to respond to each passage and to love our great and gracious God. I will recommend the Flourish series for years to come for those looking for a wise, Christ-centered study that leads toward the goal of being transformed by the word."

Taylor Turkington, Bible teacher; Director, BibleEquipping.org

"Lydia Brownback has a contagious love for the Bible. Not only is she fluent in the best of biblical scholarship in the last generation, but her writing is accessible to the simplest of readers. She has the rare ability of being clear without being reductionistic. I anticipate many women indeed will flourish through her trustworthy guidance in this series."

David Mathis, Senior Teacher and Executive Editor, desiringGod.org; Pastor, Cities Church, Saint Paul, Minnesota; author, *Habits of Grace*

LUKE

Flourish Bible Study Series
By Lydia Brownback

**FLOURISH
BIBLE STUDY**

LUKE

GOOD NEWS OF GREAT JOY

LYDIA BROWNBACK

CROSSWAY®

WHEATON, ILLINOIS

RRDS		31	30	29	28	27	26	25	24	23	22	21
14	13	12	11	10	9	8	7	6	5	4	3	2

With gratitude to God

for

Amy Kruis,
whose heart, life, and friendship regularly remind me
where true joy is found

CONTENTS

THE TIMING OF LUKE

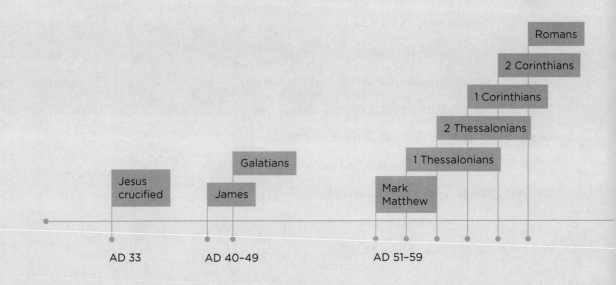

Jesus crucified

Galatians

James

Mark
Matthew

1 Thessalonians

2 Thessalonians

1 Corinthians

2 Corinthians

Romans

AD 33   AD 40-49   AD 51-59

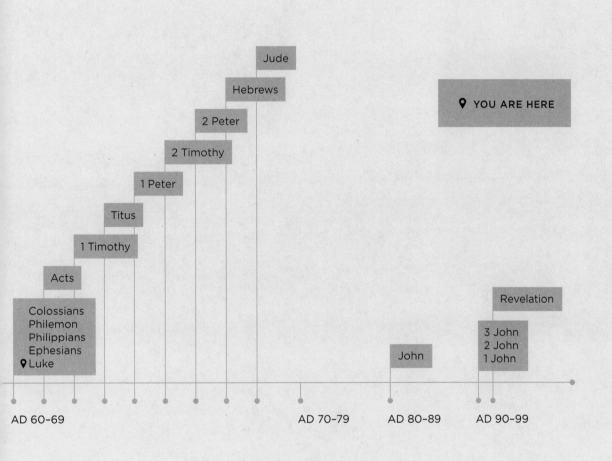

Jude

Hebrews

2 Peter

2 Timothy

1 Peter

Titus

1 Timothy

Acts

Colossians
Philemon
Philippians
Ephesians
📍 Luke

John

Revelation

3 John
2 John
1 John

📍 YOU ARE HERE

AD 60-69   AD 70-79   AD 80-89   AD 90-99

INTRODUCTION

GETTING INTO THE GOSPEL OF LUKE

Good news of great joy—that's what the angel proclaimed to some astonished shepherds one dark night in Israel. The long-awaited Messiah, the Savior promised by God, had finally come. But as time went on, people were skeptical. This man, Jesus, wasn't the sort of Savior that people had been expecting. He was an ordinary man, the son of a carpenter. He could preach a good sermon, and, yes, he was even able to heal diseases and deliver the demon possessed. Even so, how could he actually be the long-awaited King of kings that the prophets had foretold for centuries? Certainly any king sent by God would be a mighty warrior who'd instantly deliver God's people from their oppressors, right? But this Jesus was kind and gentle. He loved people and blessed them—even his enemies. And then he allowed himself to be mistreated and abused, and finally he died the most shameful kind of death—crucifixion. Many claimed to see him after he died and was raised back to life, and some actually walked and talked with him then and even joined him for a meal.

So who *is* this Jesus? That's the question Luke answers in his Gospel. But that's not all. He gives us way more than simple facts about Jesus. Luke shows us that we can believe in Jesus and entrust him with our very lives. And Jesus is worthy of our trust, as we will see. The better we know him, the longer we walk with him, the more trusting and joy-filled we'll be. In fact, life with Jesus is characterized by joy. The good news of great joy that came to the shepherds has come to us too.

WHO WAS LUKE?

Luke, the author of this Gospel, was a well-educated man with a love of history. That's clear from his writing style and from the way he has structured the material he includes. Although Luke didn't know Jesus personally, he later traveled with the apostles and spent a lot of time with the apostle Paul. This provided him the experience he needed to write not only his Gospel but also the book of Acts, which recounts how the apostles carried out the mission that had been entrusted to them by Jesus. From a

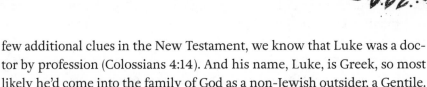

Pronunciation Guide

Barabbas: bar-AB-us

Beelzebul: BEEL-za-bull

Caesar: CEE-zer

Elijah: ill-EYE-ja

Iscariot: is-care-EE-ut

Jairus: jay-EYE-russ

Pharisees: FAIR-iss-ease

Pontius Pilate: PON-chus PIE-lit

Sadducees: SAD-you-sees

Lazarus: LAS-r-iss

Zacchaeus: za-KEY-us

Zechariah: zech-are-EYE-a

few additional clues in the New Testament, we know that Luke was a doctor by profession (Colossians 4:14). And his name, Luke, is Greek, so most likely he'd come into the family of God as a non-Jewish outsider, a Gentile. As we read his Gospel, we can tell how carefully he gathered information and conducted interviews for his writing. It's likely that he used the earlier Gospel of Mark as one of his sources, and some of Luke's content indicates that he gathered information from Jesus's mother, Mary, as well.

Luke shows, more than the other three Gospels (Matthew, Mark, and John), that Jesus had a tender heart for women. And he valued their personhood. Luke also emphasizes Jesus's compassion for the lost and lonely. "From the first announcement of his coming to his ascension into heaven, Jesus is at the center of everything: the songs are for his praise, the miracles are by his power, the teaching is from his wisdom, the conflict is over his claims, and the cross is that which only he could bear."[1]

SETTING

The events in Luke's Gospel take place in the land known as Canaan (the promised land of the Old Testament) that later became known as Palestine. The Roman Empire ruled the entire land during the events covered by Luke, and as we will see, these Roman governing authorities were part of God's plan for all that takes place in this Gospel. Jesus was raised in the town of Nazareth, and from there he ministered all over the region surrounding the Sea of Galilee. Jerusalem, the most important city in the history of God's people, is the setting for the last and most important week of Jesus's life.

The Setting of Luke[2]

---

*Marinating in the Scripture text is the most
important aspect of any Bible study.*

THEME

We can summarize the theme of Luke very simply: Jesus is the be-all-
end-all of everything.

STUDYING LUKE

In general it's good practice to read through the entire Bible passage assigned for a given week before beginning work on the study. However, some weeks in our study, especially Week 6, cover a lot of Luke's chapters. When you get to these, you might want to read the Bible passages a section at a time as you work through the lesson. However you choose to read through Luke, remember that *marinating in the Scripture text is the most important aspect of any Bible study*.

GROUP STUDY

If you are doing this study as part of a group, you'll want to finish each week's lesson before the group meeting. You can work your way through the study questions all in one sitting or by doing a little bit each day. And don't be discouraged if you don't have sufficient time to answer every question. Just do as much as you can, knowing that the more you do, the more you'll learn. No matter how much of the study you are able to complete each week, the group will benefit simply from your presence, so don't skip the gathering if you can't finish! That being said, group time will be most rewarding for every participant if you have done the lesson in advance.

If you are leading the group, you can download the free leader's guide at https://www.lydiabrownback.com/flourish-series.

INDIVIDUAL STUDY

The study is designed to run for ten weeks, but you can set your own pace if you're studying solo. And you can download the leader's guide (https://www.lydiabrownback.com/flourish-series) if you'd like some help along the way.

Reading Plan

	Primary Text	Supplemental Reading
Week 1	Luke 1:1–2:52	1 Kings 17–19; 2 Kings 1–2; 2 Samuel 7:8–16; Malachi 4:5–6; Hebrews 1:5
Week 2	Luke 3:1–4:15	Deuteronomy 8:1–3; Hebrews 4:15
Week 3	Luke 4:16–6:49	Leviticus 13
Week 4	Luke 7:1–8:56	1 Kings 17:17–24
Week 5	Luke 9:1–50	
Week 6	Luke 9:51–19:27	
Week 7	Luke 19:28–21:38	Psalms 110; 118:22; Zechariah 9:9
Week 8	Luke 22:1–71	Exodus 12:1–14
Week 9	Luke 23:1–56	Hebrews 9:1–14; 10:11–14
Week 10	Luke 24:1–53	

JOY TO THE WORLD

LUKE 1:1-2:52

Luke wants us to overcome any doubts we might have about Jesus, the God-man who came to save people from their sins. He is eager to help us experience the joy Jesus brings to all who trust in him. Even so, Luke doesn't begin his Gospel with Jesus. He begins with John the Baptist, Jesus's cousin. More accurately, he actually begins his story with the *mothers* of John and Jesus, before these two boys were even born. And then after John and Jesus are born, Luke gives us exclusive glimpses into Jesus's childhood, stories we find only in his Gospel.

1. IT REALLY HAPPENED (1:1-4)

Luke wrote his Gospel for a specific reason and addressed it to a particular person, a man named Theophilus. We don't know anything about this man, but in those days anyone referred to as "most excellent" (1:3) was someone highly respected.

✦ Where did Luke get the information for his Gospel?

_____

_____

_____

_____

✦ What reason does Luke give for writing this Gospel?

2. A LONG WAIT OVER AT LAST (1:5-25)

A godly older couple, Zechariah and Elizabeth, knew the painful ache of infertility. The child they'd always longed for hadn't come, although they'd never stopped hoping and praying for a baby. In the meantime, they trusted God and served him faithfully. But a day came when everything changed.

✦ What do we learn in this passage about the angel who spoke to Zechariah?

✦ List the details given by the angel in 1:13–17 about the child that will come to Zechariah and Elizabeth. What is so special about this child?

Gabriel tells Zechariah that his child will one day carry out a powerful and effective ministry "in the spirit and power of Elijah" (1:17). Elijah was one of the best-known Old Testament prophets (you can read about him in 1 Kings 17–19 and 2 Kings 1–2). But Gabriel isn't just making a comparison here. He's revealing something amazing: this special child was spoken about four hundred years earlier by the prophet Malachi:

> Behold, I will send you Elijah the prophet before the great and awesome day of the LORD comes. And he will turn the hearts of fathers to their children and the hearts of children to their fathers, lest I come and strike the land with a decree of utter destruction. (Malachi 4:5–6)

Can you see Malachi's prophecy reflected in the angel's promise to Zechariah? This baby—who grows up to become John the Baptist—was sent to get people ready for the coming Messiah. That was the whole point of his ministry.

✤ Why was Zechariah unable to speak after his encounter with Gabriel, and where do we see evidence of this in his conversation with the angel?

The Angel Gabriel

Angels like Gabriel are God's messengers. Gabriel is one of only two in the Bible to be named (the other is Michael). Gabriel brings a message to Daniel in the Old Testament (Daniel 8:16), and returns to visit him in "swift flight" (Daniel 9:21). When Gabriel brings Zechariah God's message here in Luke, we learn that Gabriel stands in the presence of God, and Gabriel is also the angel who explains to Mary that she will bear the Son of God.

---

3. NOTHING IS IMPOSSIBLE FOR GOD (1:26–56)

When Zechariah's wife, Elizabeth, quietly rejoices over the baby growing in her womb, her relative Mary receives a visit from the angel Gabriel. She too, like Zechariah before her, is promised a son, and just like Zechariah, she's a bit distressed at first. After all, Mary is young, probably thirteen or fourteen, and not yet officially married, although she was engaged to a man named Joseph.

✦ List from 1:32–33 the five things Gabriel tells Mary about the son she will bear.

1. ....

2. ....

3. ....

4. ....

5. ....

It's likely that Mary had grown up hearing about the history of her Jewish ancestors. If so, she would have heard that the most famous one of all, the great Old Testament King David, had been promised an heir who would one day restore freedom and peace to God's people and rule the world forever with power and love:

> Your house and your kingdom shall be made sure forever before me. Your throne shall be established forever. (2 Samuel 7:16)

If Mary knew of this promise, no wonder she was utterly shocked by Gabriel's words—this long-awaited king is to be *her* son?

✦ How does the angel answer Mary's question about how she'll conceive this special baby, and how does Mary respond?

....

....

....

....

....

....

....

Joy Note

Elizabeth is promised joy as God ends her barrenness and unfolds his plans for this long-awaited son (Luke 1:14). *God's answers to our prayers are meant to bring joy.*

✦ Learning from Gabriel that her older relative Elizabeth is also carrying a baby, Mary hurries to visit her. What happens when Mary enters Elizabeth's home, and what does Elizabeth say to Mary?

✦ After hearing Elizabeth's joyful words, the amazed Mary can't help but break out in praise and worship. The song she sings (1:46–55) is called the "Magnificat" because her lyrics *magnify* the Lord. What reasons does she give in 1:48–49 for her rejoicing?

✦ Something we will see in Luke is how God reverses things. He turns things around and does the unexpected. God does this to show human beings that he controls everything and everyone. What reversals do you see in Mary's song?

✦ At the end of her song, Mary comes back to the wonder of the baby she is carrying and that this child is the fulfillment of God's longtime promise going all the way back to David's ancestor Abraham. What does 1:54 reveal about God's purpose for this baby?

4. A VERY HAPPY DAY (1:57–80)

At long last Elizabeth gives birth to a son. Friends and family rejoice, and, as was the custom in those days, they all come together eight days later for the baby's circumcision, which marked the child as belonging to God and his people Israel. Those gathered for the ceremony assume the boy will be named for his father, Zechariah, but Elizabeth tells them no, the boy's name will be John.

✦ Months before, Zechariah's unbelief had closed his ears and tongue (1:18–20). What act of faith opens them back up again here?

✦ How do friends and relatives respond to the naming of the baby and what happens to Zechariah?

Luke tells us that Zechariah is filled with the Holy Spirit, which lets us know that the words he's about to say are a prophecy from the Lord. (The same thing happened with Elizabeth back in 1:41–42.) Although Zechariah is rejoicing over the birth of his son, his heart is even more captivated by his promise-keeping God. Zechariah praises, or blesses, God because he has "visited and redeemed his people" (1:68). Zechariah is speaking here not of his own son, John, but of the son Mary will bear—Jesus. He is the "horn of salvation" raised up from the line of King David (1:69). He is the one foretold long ago by the prophets.

✝ According to the remaining verses in Zechariah's prophecy, what will this "horn of salvation" accomplish for God's people?

· 1:71

· 1:72–73

· 1:74–75

✝ After rejoicing in God's goodness to his people, Zechariah begins talking about his own son, John. What does he foretell about John in 1:76–77?

✤ The Savior is coming, and God wants people to know! And that's what God has in mind for John—to get people ready for Jesus. What does the imagery in 1:78–79 reveal about this Savior to come?

....

....

....

....

5. THE LORD HAS COME! (2:1–21)

Here for the first time we meet Joseph, the man Mary is engaged to marry. An engagement, or betrothal, in those days was almost as binding as an actual marriage. Joseph takes Mary, now supernaturally pregnant with the promised child, to his hometown of Bethlehem, which had also been the hometown of the great Old Testament King David. (Luke wants us to notice the connection to King David here. It's actually an important part of the story.) Traveling wasn't easy in those days, especially for a pregnant woman, but the government had issued a decree that required them to make the trip at this inconvenient time.

The government seemed to be directing the course of Joseph and Mary, but actually it was God. He was the one guiding all these circumstances to fulfill a promise he'd made long ago, that Mary's baby, the Messiah, would be born in Bethlehem (Micah 5:2). And sure enough—Mary went into labor while they were there. The town was so crowded with visitors that lodging was hard to find, and they had no choice but to deliver Mary's baby among farm animals, in uncomfortable and unsanitary conditions.

Joy Note

The shepherds are promised that the arrival of Jesus is meant to bring joy to all people (Luke 2:10). *Turning to Jesus for salvation is the path to increasing joy that never ends.*

But you, O Bethlehem Ephrathah,
who are too little to be among the clans of Judah,
from you shall come forth for me
one who is to be ruler in Israel,
whose coming forth is from of old,
from ancient days. (Micah 5:2)

✟ Meanwhile, a gathering of on-duty shepherds was spending the night in an open field under the stars. Suddenly an angel appeared, frightening them out of their wits. What did the angel tell the shepherds?

✟ What do the shepherds do and say after this heavenly encounter?

"Everything we know about the birth of Jesus points
to obscurity, indignity, pain, and rejection. One of the
great mysteries of the universe is that when God the Son
became a man he spent his first night in a barn."[3]

6. WORTH WAITING FOR (2:22-40)

Forty days later, Mary and Joseph take the baby Jesus up to the temple in Jerusalem to dedicate him to the Lord. This ceremony was a requirement under Jewish law for all firstborn sons. While Mary and Joseph are there, they encounter two people in the temple—a man named Simeon and an elderly woman, Anna. Both have been watching and waiting for this miracle baby.

✦ What does Simeon prophesy about the baby Jesus and about Mary?

....

....

....

....

✦ What does Anna do when she discovers the baby Jesus?

....

....

....

....

7. A WISE BOY (2:39-52)

Luke is the only Gospel writer to give us a glimpse of Jesus as a boy. It's here that we see Jesus thrive both physically and spiritually and that the hand of God is watching over him. When Jesus is twelve years old, he makes a decisive change in the way he relates to his family.

✦ What choice does Jesus make that distresses and baffles his parents?

....

....

....

....

✦ Here in 2:51 and also back in 2:19, Luke tells us that Mary "treasured" in her heart the happenings in and around her son. What does this seem to convey about Mary?

LET'S TALK

1. Zechariah was unable to hear or speak for several months because he doubted God's word, but "God disciplined him in a way that taught him to trust. This is something God often does, and it is always a mercy when he does it. He uses the hard experience of suffering to teach us to trust in him."[4] Describe a time in your life when God used a painful circumstance to deepen your faith.

2. What emotions most characterize the people in these opening chapters as they experience startling changes and unexpected circumstances? Consider Zechariah, Elizabeth, Mary, the shepherds, Simeon, and Anna. How has your relationship with the Lord most noticeably

impacted you? Consider not just emotions, but also thoughts, decisions, and circumstances.

3. Anna's life was reshaped at a young age by the death of her husband. How has God worked in some unexpected circumstance to reshape your life? How have you tended to respond to the Lord's unexpected—and perhaps unwanted—providences?

GET READY!

LUKE 3:1-4:15

Zechariah and Elizabeth's son John is now a full-grown man, and he's ready to carry out the special ministry he'd been destined for—getting people ready for the arrival of the long-awaited Savior. John soon becomes well known, as he travels around telling people about Jesus—who he is and what he will do. But then John is unjustly thrown in prison, and he fades into the background so that Jesus takes center stage. As Luke brings Jesus to the forefront, we soon discover that Jesus is no ordinary human being. As Mary's son, he is human, but as God's Son, he is also divine. Jesus is the only person in history to have both a divine nature and a human nature. And people begin to wonder, Who *is* this unique man?

1. HEARTS PREPARED (3:1-20)

John is living in the wilderness when he receives God's call. The time has come for John to spread the word. The Savior is here! As a good historian, Luke is careful to give us details about the region where John is going to carry out his ministry, and that includes identifying the local authorities. We won't take a detailed look at these authorities here (but take a look at the chart on the next page). For now, suffice it to say that there were some sketchy characters among them. At the top is Tiberius Caesar, the head over all the Roman Empire. Under him is a governor named Pontius Pilate. He oversees the region where Luke's story takes place. And then there are the Herods, more localized rulers called "tetrarchs." Luke also identifies two religious authorities,

Jewish and Roman Rulers[5]

Date	Roman Emperors	Roman Prefects/Procurators of Judea and Samaria	Roman Prefects/ Procurators of All Israel	Herodian Dynasty (37 B.C.–A.D. 93)
40 B.C.				
30 B.C.	Augustus (31 B.C.–A.D. 14)			Herod the Great (37 B.C.–4 B.C.)
20 B.C.				
10 B.C.				
A.D. 2				Philip (4 B.C.–A.D. 34)
A.D. 10		Coponius (A.D. 6–9) Marcus Ambibulus (A.D. 9–12) Annius Rufus (A.D. 12–15)		
A.D. 20	Tiberius (A.D. 14–37)	Valerius Gratus (A.D. 15–26)		
A.D. 30		Pontius Pilate (A.D. 26–36/37)		
A.D. 40		Marcellus (A.D. 36/37) Marullus (A.D. 37–41)		Agrippa I (A.D. 37, 41–44)
A.D. 50	Gaius (A.D. 37–41) Claudius (A.D. 41–54)		Fadus (A.D. 44–46) Tiberius Alexander (A.D. 44–46) Ventidius Cumanus (A.D. 48–52)	Agrippa II (A.D. 44–92/93)
A.D. 60	Nero (A.D. 54–68)		Felix (A.D. 52–60) Porcius Festus (A.D. 60–62) Albinus (A.D. 62–64)	
A.D. 70	Galba/Otho/Vitellius (A.D. 68) Vespasian (A.D. 69–79)		Gesius Florus (A.D. 64–66)	
A.D. 80	Titus (A.D. 79–81)			
A.D. 90	Domitian (A.D. 81–96)			
A.D. 100	Nerva (A.D. 96–98)			
A.D. 110	Trajan (A.D. 98–117)			
A.D. 120				
A.D. 130	Hadrian (A.D. 117–138)			
A.D. 140				
A.D. 150	Antonius Pius (A.D. 138–161)			
A.D. 160				
	Marcus Aurelius (A.D. 161–180) with Lucius Verus (A.D. 161–180)			

Date	Herodian Dynasty (37 B.C.–A.D. 93)		Jewish High Priests	
40 B.C.				
30 B.C.				
20 B.C.				
10 B.C.				
A.D. 2	Archelaus *(4 B.C.–A.D. 6)*	Antipas *(4 B.C.–A.D. 39)*	Joazar son of Boethus *(4 B.C.)* Jesus son of Sie *(3 B.C.–A.D. 6)*	Eleazar son of Boethus *(4 B.C.–?)*
A.D. 10			Annas *(A.D. 6-15)* Ishmael son of Phiabi *(A.D. 15-16)*	
A.D. 20			Eleazar son of Annas *(A.D. 16–17)* Simon son of Camithus *(A.D. 17–18)*	
A.D. 30				Josephus Caiaphas son-in-law of Annas *(A.D. 18–36)*
A.D. 40			Jonathan son of Annas *(A.D. 36–37)* Simon Cantheras son of Boethus *(A.D. 41)* Elionaeus son of Cantheras *(A.D. 44–46)*	Theophilus son of Annas *(A.D. 37–41)* Matthias son of Annas *(A.D. 41–44)*
A.D. 50			Ananias son of Nedebaeus *(A.D. 47-58)*	
A.D. 60				
			Ananus son of Annas *(A.D. 62)*	
A.D. 70				
A.D. 80				
A.D. 90				
A.D. 100				
A.D. 110				
A.D. 120				
A.D. 130				
A.D. 140				
A.D. 150				
A.D. 160				

the high priests Annas and Caiaphas, who have no civil authority but regulate God's people in their worship of God.

So out of the wilderness comes John, this rather odd man, preaching about Jesus Christ to all who will listen. And people do listen! Some who encounter John realize that he's the one identified by Isaiah the prophet centuries earlier—the announcer, the herald, of the good news for all who put their trust in God.

✦ What does John tell the people, and what tone does he take in 3:8–9?

....

....

....

....

✦ John has a special criticism for those who think their religious ancestry—their connection to the Old Testament patriarch Abraham—makes them right with God. As you consider his strong words in verses 8–9, what point is John making?

....

....

....

....

✦ Many in the crowds take John's message to heart. They come to him to repent of their sin, and they let John baptize them in the Jordan River. (This is why he's called John *the Baptist*.) And as the people come, John outlines specific ways they must change. What do all these requirements that John names in 3:11–14 have in common?

....

....

....

....

✦ John is clearly having an impact, and people's hearts are stirred by all he's saying and doing. In fact, he's proving to be such a powerful influence that some begin to wonder if perhaps he himself might actually be the Savior. So in 3:16–17, what does John tell the people about himself and about Jesus?

John "preached good news to the people" (3:18). We might wonder how Luke can speak of "good news," seeing as how John talks so much about sin and guilt. But that's actually the whole point. We do have much sin to repent of, and even when we manage to clean up our conduct and vow to do better, we can't change our heart's inclination to keep on sinning. But the good news, the gospel, is that Jesus has come to do exactly that—make us clean from the inside out.

✦ What brings an end to John's preaching ministry?

✦ What does Luke reveal in this section about the character of Herod?

2. SON OF GOD, SON OF MAN (LUKE 3:21-38)

John's ministry of announcing Jesus the Messiah comes to an abrupt halt, but before that happens, he baptizes Jesus. We have to wonder why Jesus, who was completely sinless, agreed to be baptized, since baptism symbolizes cleansing from sin. The reason is, he did it to identify with us, his sinful people. By getting baptized, Jesus entered into our experience, our need to be washed from our sinfulness. And this act at the beginning of his public life points ahead to what he will do at the end, when he will take the full weight of our sin on himself at the cross.

Herod

Herod had fallen in love with Herodias, the wife of his half brother Philip. Herod also was married at the time. Herod and Herodias both divorced their spouses in order to marry each other. But John the Baptist spoke out publicly against this immoral union.

✤ What happens next, in 3:22, marks the beginning of Jesus's public ministry. God is present here in three persons—Father, Son, and Holy Spirit. Where do you see all three persons, the Trinity, in this amazing event?

· Father:

· Son:

· Holy Spirit:

....

....

When we want to know something about our ancestors, we sign up for one of those online services that traces our personal history using the DNA we provide from a Q-tip swab of our cheek. In Bible times, they relied on good historians like Luke to compile someone's background information. That's exactly what Luke does in this section, giving us the genealogy of Jesus. While certainly not every relative of Jesus is included here, those Luke does choose to include are meant to show Jesus's connection to King David (3:31).

✦ How far back in history does Luke trace Jesus's ancestry?

....

....

....

....

As we leave Luke 3, reflect for a moment on what Luke has shown us in this chapter about the person of Jesus. He is the beloved Son of the heavenly Father (3:22) but also the descendant of a long line of men. Luke really wants us to get that Jesus is both divine and human.

3. TRIED AND TEMPTED (4:1-15)

Jesus has now been baptized and anointed by the Holy Spirit to go forward with his mission, but before he begins, he's led into the wilderness for forty days of intense personal testing by the devil.

✦ Jesus fasted for this entire forty days, which is just about the limit a human being can survive with no food. The devil, well aware of Jesus's extreme hunger, points out how easily Jesus could fill his empty stomach. Jesus answers with a quote from the Old Testament, Deuteronomy 8:3, which he'd likely been thinking about during the long, lonely days in the wilderness. Read Deuteronomy 8:1–3 and note why it's a good passage for fighting against the devil's temptation.

....

....

✧ Another time the devil "showed him all the kingdoms of the world in a moment of time" (4:5). Here we are given a glimpse into a realm that is barred from us—the future. The two of them, Jesus and the devil, stand looking into the future, all the way to the end of time. What is the devil seeking from Jesus with this particular temptation?

✧ For the time being, the devil has great power in this world, as he says in 4:6, but even that is totally controlled by God. As the devil tries to tempt Jesus once again, Jesus continues to resist him. What does this forty-day season in Jesus's life teach us about God's word?

"Jesus and Satan squared off in the wilderness. This takes us back to the place where the Israelites wandered, not for forty days, but for forty years. Just as the children of Israel were tested, so also Jesus—the true Israel—would be tested in the wilderness. There he would do what God's people had failed to do: live in grateful obedience to God."[6]

We noted earlier that Jesus was baptized in order to identify with us, his people. And this same need to identify with us is a huge part of these forty days of temptation. The New Testament letter of Hebrews tells us that Jesus is able to sympathize with our weaknesses because he too was tempted, even though he never once gave in (Hebrews 4:15). That's why we can turn to him when we're tempted to sin or after we've given into temptation. He understands. And not only that—his victory over temptation covers each and every one of our failures.

> *We do not have a high priest who is unable to sympathize with our weaknesses, but one who in every respect has been tempted as we are, yet without sin. Let us then with confidence draw near to the throne of grace, that we may receive mercy and find grace to help in time of need. (Hebrews 4:15–16)*

The devil finally leaves Jesus, at least for the time being, and Jesus comes out of the wilderness into the region of Galilee, ready to begin in full all he'd come to earth to do.

LET'S TALK

1. Name a specific time when God's word strengthened you against temptation or guided you in an important decision or transformed your heart in some way. Jesus knew God's word so well that he could draw from it in a moment of great need. Identify some practical ways we can make it just as readily available in our own minds and hearts so that we can apply it to our circumstances continually.

....

....

....

....

2. As you consider the three specific temptations Jesus experienced in the wilderness, identify which one might be a particular temptation for you. Is it the temptation to gratify your cravings in sinful ways, or to seek glory for yourself in who you are and what you do, or to demand that God prove himself to you by answering prayers on your own terms or timetable? Discuss the Bible passages Jesus used as a means of fighting temptation and any others that might be helpful for you in a current struggle.

....

....

....

....

....

....

....

....

IS HE FOR REAL?

LUKE 4:16-6:49

As Jesus makes himself known, first in his hometown of Nazareth and then throughout the region of Galilee, people take notice. There's something compelling about this man showing up to teach in the local synagogues. More astonishing still are his miracles, which generate excitement and great curiosity and draw great crowds. So when he singles out a few men to join up with him, they gladly come along. Even so, others hate him, especially the religious leaders because what Jesus is saying and doing diminishes their own authority.

1. LEAVING HOME (4:16-30)

Surely Jesus had a heart for his hometown, the familiar surroundings of Nazareth where he and his siblings had grown up together. So quite naturally, he comes here to preach the good news of the gospel, and he does so in the neighborhood synagogue. Like all good preachers, Jesus anchors his message in God's word, and here he uses the words of Isaiah the Old Testament prophet. Centuries before, Isaiah had described what the Messiah would be like and what he would do. We can't help but wonder if the people listening to Jesus in the synagogue realize that Jesus, in citing Isaiah, was actually preaching about himself!

Jesus's Ministry in Galilee[7]

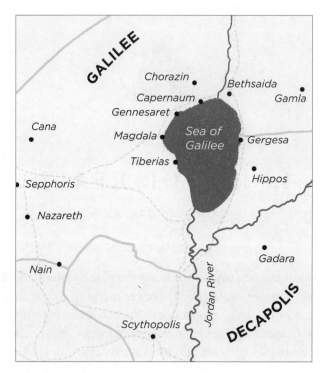

✦ According to Luke 4:18–19 (which is a quote from Isaiah), what is the Messiah's mission, and who is he sent to save?

The locals were all impressed by Jesus's eloquent teaching, but they didn't embrace his message. This son of a carpenter—the Messiah? They find the idea preposterous, so they demand proof. If Jesus will just do a miracle, they'll believe him. But Jesus refuses to give in to the crowd's demands. Instead, he reminds them of God's people from Old Testament days who missed God's blessings because they wouldn't believe. The crowd wants it the other way around: "Show us, and then we will believe!" But their demand is actually *un-belief*, and Jesus won't meet them on those terms. Instead, just as in Old Testament days, he will take his blessings elsewhere. This gets the crowd so angry that they run Jesus out of his hometown to the edge of a cliff, where they try to his push him to his death. Somehow he escapes, and then he goes to Capernaum, a city in the region of Galilee.

2. DEMONS AND DISEASE (4:31-44)

Jesus's fame grows as he travels around teaching God's word and preaching the good news of salvation. But not only does Jesus preach—he practices what he preaches, healing the sick and freeing people living in bondage to the forces of evil.

✢ While Jesus was teaching in the Capernaum synagogue, he was confronted by a demon-possessed man (4:31–37). What does the watching crowd learn about the demon and about Jesus during this encounter?

_____

_____

_____

_____

After this miraculous deliverance, Jesus leaves the synagogue and goes to the home of a man named Simon, who we will come to know as Peter. Jesus has come to the home of this friend, perhaps seeking some rest and refreshment. Yet all is not peaceful at Peter's house because Peter's mother-in-law has a dangerously high fever. In great distress, the family seeks Jesus's help, and Jesus heals her instantly. When word of this gets out, the sick and troubled line up to get near Jesus. Even though he is surely tired, he lays his hands on each and every one and heals them. He banishes demons too, and then forbids the demons to reveal his identity. Jesus will reveal who he is in his own way and time.

3. FISHERS OF MEN (5:1-11)

Another day, another crowd. People come from all over Galilee to hear Jesus teach and to see—perhaps even receive—a miracle. On one occasion, while Jesus is teaching at water's edge, a crowd presses in so close that he has to jump into a nearby boat to get some breathing room. The boat is familiar to Jesus because it belongs to Simon Peter, who is a fisherman by trade. Jesus finishes his sermon from the safety of the boat, and then he centers his attention on Peter and a few other men fishing in nearby boats.

✦ How does Peter's view of Jesus change after the miraculous catch of fish?

✦ Peter's response to Jesus after the miraculous catch might seem a bit odd at first. We'd expect Peter to simply pour out praise and amazement for this display of divine power. Instead, Peter expresses a desire to get away from Jesus (5:8). What causes Peter to feel this way?

✦ In what way does the large catch of fish reveal to the astonished men the calling Jesus has planned for them?

✦ What do Peter, James, and John do when they get back onshore?

4. FAITH, FORGIVENESS, AND FULLNESS OF LIFE (5:12–26)

Luke wants us to see that Jesus heals all kinds of people in all kinds of circumstances. One time, a man stricken with leprosy falls on the ground in front of Jesus and begs to be healed—a really bold move because lepers were social outcasts and were required to keep socially distant from others. It took a lot of courage for this man to fall before Jesus and make his request. And Jesus quickly and gladly heals him—not just with a word but also with a touch. The man likely hasn't felt human touch for a long time.

✦ Seeing Jesus's willingness to heal the leper emboldens more people to come forward. After all, if he'd been willing to touch a leper, then wouldn't he be willing to help them too? And Jesus does. How, according to verse 16, does Jesus find refreshment in the midst of ministering to so many?

> ### Leprosy
>
> Leprosy in the Bible includes more than just the disease we call Hansen's disease today. In Bible times "leprosy" included a variety of skin infections and ailments such as psoriasis. Fear of contagion caused those with these skin problems to be shunned by society, and Old Testament laws required sufferers to warn others by crying out, "Unclean!" To be a leper was a painful, isolating experience.

Another healing happens in the middle of a teaching session, when Jesus is speaking to a group of religious bigwigs who had come from all over the region to hear him. As he speaks, an astonishing sight comes into view. A paralyzed man, lying on a bed that's suspended on ropes of some sort, is descending from the ceiling and comes to rest directly in front of Jesus. Needless to say, his sermon was instantly disrupted.

✦ What does Jesus say when he sees this bold act?

....

....

....

....

✦ What reason does Jesus give for healing the paralyzed man?

....

....

....

....

5. AN UNLIKELY CONVERT (5:27–32)

Tax collectors in Jesus's day were viewed with a measure of both fear and contempt, much like we view financial charlatans who scheme ways to bilk the unsuspecting and vulnerable out of their life savings. For that reason, there's likely a good bit of shock and dismay when Jesus calls a tax collector named Levi to come join his band of disciples.

✦ Levi was overjoyed to be singled out by this well-known teacher and miracle worker, and he honors Jesus with a dinner party in gratitude. The disciples come to the feast, as do lots of Levi's tax-collecting friends. But some religious leaders, the Pharisees, look down their noses at the occasion. After all, they think, Jesus couldn't be all that great if he hangs out with the likes of Levi. What do we learn about Jesus's mission from what he says to the Pharisees?

....

....

....

....

Religious Leaders in Jesus's Day		
Pharisees	**Sadducees**	**Scribes**
• Tried to shape Jewish religious life • Held in high regard • Sought to please God through good works	• Came from wealthy families • Known as unfriendly • Did not believe in resurrection	• Preachers in local synagogues

6. OUT WITH THE OLD, IN WITH THE NEW (5:33-39)

The Pharisees continue to press Jesus with demanding questions—not because they really want to know the answers but because they want to bring him down. They resent his popularity and his claims. Jesus sees right through them, of course, so he answers them indirectly, speaking in parables. When the Pharisees accuse him of leading his disciples astray, away from religious regulations like fasting, he makes clear that his presence with them is a time for joy, not fasting. A time for fasting will come later, he tells them. He is hinting here at the end of his life, the coming crucifixion.

A parable is a story or word picture designed to teach a lesson.

✦ And then Jesus tells them a parable. He wants the Pharisees to picture in their minds two garments, one new and one old, and then the same with two wineskins. According to Jesus, what happens when someone tries to bind the old and the new together?

The point of Jesus's parable is that the old religious ways—keeping the strict rules and regulations that have governed God's people all through the Old Testament—are changing now that the Messiah, Jesus, has come.

7. LORD OF THE LAW (6:1–11)

The Old Testament law—the rules and regulations—was never supposed to be a depressing burden for God's people. God had given them the law to bless them. One of those good laws had to do with setting aside one day a week, the Sabbath day, for rest and worshiping the Lord. Over time, however, this blessing of the Sabbath had become a crushing burden because the Pharisees hovered over its every little detail, dictating what people could and could not do. So, for example, looking in a mirror was forbidden, because one might see a gray hair and be tempted to pluck it out, and the Pharisees said that plucking was "work." So God's good gift of the Sabbath was being abused.

✛ The Pharisees catch Jesus and his disciples plucking grain to eat as a snack on the Sabbath and call them out, but Jesus silences them with a good story from the Old Testament. And then on another Sabbath, Jesus heals a man—also forbidden. By doing these activities on Sabbath days, what is Jesus communicating about how his coming has changed the old ways?

....

....

....

....

✛ Why do you think Jesus's teaching on the Sabbath makes the Pharisees so angry?

....

....

....

....

8. SET APART (6:12–16)

From among his many disciples, Jesus chose twelve to carry out a special mission—they were to be apostles. The term *apostle* means "messenger" or "one who is sent out." These twelve apostles would travel around with Jesus and learn from his teaching, and then later, when Jesus would no longer be with them, they would devote their lives to taking his message everywhere they possibly could. Peter heads the list of the twelve, and we find Jesus's other two best friends here as well—James and John. There's also Levi the tax collector, called "Matthew" here. And last on the list is Judas, who, as we will see, is a dark and tragic figure.

✦ What did Jesus do the night before choosing the apostles?

9. RESTING ON ROCK (6:17–49)

Jesus frequently taught outdoors, and we have a prime instance here in this section, where Luke records a sermon Jesus preached from a large open area, a plain.

✦ Jesus wants everyone to know what life is like in the kingdom of God, the life he gives to people who put their faith in him. Those who enter in find that hardships and difficulties get turned into blessings. List the reversals you see in 6:20–22, a section of the sermon that theologians call "the Beatitudes," which comes from a Latin word that means "blessed."

· 6:20

· 6:21

· 6:22

Those who refuse to trust Jesus not only miss the blessings of God's kingdom; they experience the opposite—woe. Jesus says in 6:24–26 that people who look for fulfillment in what this world has to offer—riches and pleasures and reputation—will regret it in the long run.

✟ Loving people is hard sometimes, isn't it? That can be true even with those we're closest to. Hardest of all, of course, is loving those who have hurt us. Yet that's the very thing Jesus instructs us to do. How is this possible? It's not, unless we're disciples of Jesus, living in him by faith. Then the Holy Spirit transforms us to be able to love this way. How does Jesus describe real love in 6:27–36?

Jesus's talk about love flows naturally to the topic of judging people (6:37–38), and he calls his followers to believe the best about others. He's not talking about a naïve blindness, a refusal to face unpleasant realities about people and about sin. (Elsewhere God's word calls us to be discerning about such things.[8]) Jesus has in mind here a generosity of spirit toward people and in how we assess what they do. God is pleased when we are willing to view others this way, and he will bless us for it.

✦ Jesus reinforces his teaching here with a parable in 6:39–42. How would you summarize the lesson of this parable?

....

....

....

....

....

....

....

Joy Note

Jesus taught that being hated for his sake brings joy because rewards for this kind of suffering are guaranteed (Luke 6:23). *Jesus notices when we are rejected for our faith, and he promises to bless us for remaining faithful.*

✦ Jesus concludes this topic—judging others and humbly assessing ourselves and others—with a metaphor about fruit trees. He is equipping his followers to be discerning. What do these fruit trees show us about how to discern?

....

....

....

....

✦ Jesus wraps up his sermon with a warning in 6:46–49. What is that warning?

....

....

....

....

LET'S TALK

1. Review Jesus's description of love in 6:27–36. Where has such love seemed most difficult—if not downright impossible—for you? Given that the Lord promises to help us, the big question is, are we willing? Consider the implications for your own life.

2. One reason the Pharisees hated Jesus is that he accepted and healed people who, in their eyes, weren't worthy. Consider how you respond when the undeserving receive a great blessing. Do you rejoice in the amazing mercy of God, or are you sometimes more like the Pharisees? Try to identify a recent example.

THE COMPASSIONATE SAVIOR

LUKE 7:1-8:56

Jesus has a tender heart for women. We see it in his compassion for the lonely and hurting and in how he befriends women and dignifies their personhood. Something else we see, as Jesus travels around the region of Galilee, is how much he values humility and love. In fact, he so clearly wants the hearts of people even more than their good deeds. This week John the Baptist comes back into the story again, but on a somber note because he's struggling with doubt. But as we'll see, Jesus is able to overcome anyone's doubts.

1. A POWERFUL MAN'S PLEA (7:1–10)

Jesus's ears are always open to earnest pleas, which is exactly the case with a group of Jewish elders who have come to ask Jesus to help a friend of theirs, a Roman official. This official was a centurion, which means he had charge of one hundred Roman soldiers. And although he wasn't Jewish, and therefore not one of God's people, he'd been a Jewish supporter, and he'd even donated some of his wealth to build them a synagogue. So it's understandable that these grateful elders are eager to help him. The problem was, for all the centurion's wealth and status, he was powerless to heal his sick servant, one who clearly meant a great deal to him. But he'd heard of Jesus and his miraculous healings, and he got his hopes up. Jesus listens to this story and then follows the elders toward the centurion's residence, but they are stopped along the way by a messenger bringing word from the centurion himself.

✦ What message does the centurion send to Jesus?

....

....

....

....

✦ How does Jesus respond to the message, and what does he do?

....

....

....

....

2. DO NOT WEEP (7:11–17)

Jesus comes to a town called Nain, and just on the outskirts he encounters wailing and distraught mourners in the midst of a funeral procession. Jesus quickly discerns that the most grieved of the mourners is the mother of the deceased. Already a widow, she is now left alone in the world without her only son.

✦ What compels Jesus to speak to the widow and help her?

....

....

....

....

✦ What does Jesus do after he raises the dead man?

....

....

....

....

The crowd is astonished, and all the people praise God with shouts of glory, and they say, "A great prophet has arisen among us!" (7:16). The miracle reminds them of an Old Testament event, a time when the prophet Elijah had raised a widow's son and reunited that son with his grieving mother (you can read the story in 1 Kings 17:17–24). Luke wants us to understand that Jesus is the greater Elijah—the ultimate and final prophet sent by God to speak God's words.

Widows in Luke
• Anna in the temple (2:37) • Widow of Zarephath (4:25-26) • Widow whose only son died (7:12) • Widow who persisted (18:3-5) • Fictitious widow with seven husbands (20:28) • Widows mistreated in the name of religion (20:47) • Poor widow who sacrifices (21:2-3)

3. DOUBTING JOHN (7:18-35)

It's been a long time since we've heard from John the Baptist. Last we knew, he'd been thrown in prison by Herod. That's where he still is, languishing in prison, and he sends two of his own disciples to ask Jesus an important question: "Are you the one who is to come, or shall we look for another?" (7:19). It seems that John is having doubts. Was this Jesus, his very own cousin—the one he'd devoted his life to preaching about—really the Messiah? Because it sure didn't look that way. Wasn't the promised one supposed to be a king like the great King David of old? This man Jesus just travels around preaching and keeping questionable company sometimes, and while he draws great crowds with his teaching and miracles, he just doesn't seem, well, very kingly.

✢ What does Jesus do and say in 7:21–23 in response to John's inquiry?

_____

_____

_____

_____

Jesus's last remark carries a bit of rebuke. It seems that John has been expecting a messiah who'd display great feats of military might, putting the arrogant Romans in their place and restoring the Jewish people to the worldwide domination they'd enjoyed a thousand years before. So, John wonders, could this humble, gentle man really be the promised one? We certainly can have compassion on doubting John. He'd taken a stand for truth and carried out his God-given calling, only to wind up in a prison cell.

John's people take their leave of Jesus, and then Jesus talks about John to those gathered around. True, John may have been a bit odd, Jesus says. Even so, John is the greatest prophet of all time. Not only did John get to announce the arrival of the Messiah; he got to baptize him as well. Even so, Jesus says, anyone who believes in Jesus and enters by faith into the new life he's bringing is actually more privileged than the greatest prophet. That's because all the prophets, including John, carried out their ministries before Jesus was fully revealed. It is we—believers who know of his life, death, and resurrection—who see in full. And therefore we are more blessed than John the Baptist and all those who lived before Jesus finished his earthly mission (7:24–30).

Finally, Jesus speaks a sharp word to the religious leaders out there in the crowd, those who refuse to believe the words of either John or Jesus. Those who refuse are like whining children who make petty and false allegations against those they don't like (7:31–35).

4. A LESSON FOR SCORNFUL SIMON (7:36-50)

One of the Pharisees, a man named Simon, actually invites Jesus to his home for dinner, which is where we next find Jesus. In those days people ate lying on their side, supported by an elbow, head near the table, and feet stretched out behind them. That's how an unknown woman finds Jesus when she enters the room.

✟ What does Luke tell us about this woman?

....

....

....

....

The woman, overcome with emotion, stands behind Jesus and anoints his feet with ointment, an act of hospitality in those days. The Pharisee host watches the unfolding scene with contempt, but Jesus knows the thoughts of the Pharisee and gently instructs him.

✦ What does Jesus reveal about this woman's heart?

_____

_____

_____

_____

✦ What happens to the woman—and why?

_____

_____

_____

_____

✦ What does Jesus reveal about himself on this occasion?

_____

_____

_____

_____

5. MARY MAGDALENE AND MANY MORE (8:1-3)

Jesus, eager to share the good news of God's kingdom, moves frequently from town to town. His twelve special disciples travel with him, and, as Luke tells us here, so do a handful of women.

✦ He mentions three of these women by name: Mary Magdalene, Joanna, and Susanna. They come from different backgrounds, but what, according to 8:2, do these three women hold in common?

_____

_____

....

....

....

....

✦ What do the women do for Jesus as they travel with him and his inner circle of disciples?

....

....

....

....

....

....

....

....

....

> ### Mary Magdalene
>
> Mary was called Magdalene because she was from Magdala, a city on the western shore of Galilee. She committed her life to Jesus after he delivered her from a multitude of demons. Mary was present when Jesus was crucified. Afterward, when he'd been raised from death, Jesus appeared to Mary before anyone else.

Luke gives a good bit of attention to the women in Jesus's world. He wants us to see that women matter to Jesus—he values them as friends and as disciples, and he cares not only about what they do but also about what they think. As one commentator tells us, "Jesus wanted to do more for these women than forgive their sins: he wanted to disciple their minds."[9]

6. GOOD FRUIT, BRIGHT LIGHT, AND THE FAMILY OF FAITH (8:4–21)

Luke gives us more of Jesus's teaching, and he starts off here with a parable about seeds planted in different types of soil.

✦ Identify the four types of soil and what happens to the seeds that fall in each type:

1. ....

2. ....

3. ....

4. ....

✦ According to 8:9–10, why does Jesus speak in parables?

....

....

....

....

Jesus's explanation of the parables seems shocking, doesn't it? It's meant to shock us, and it serves as a warning that those who reject the gospel message—salvation in Jesus Christ alone—harden their hearts toward him so that, if they persist in refusing him, they can no longer see or hear anything he says.

After the parable, Jesus uses the image of a lamp to illustrate a vital aspect of living the Christian life. His point is that those truly in God's kingdom, those united to Christ by faith, delight to show the light of Jesus to others. Some who see the light will believe; others won't. And sooner or later, the truth about everyone's heart will be known. Jesus is hinting here at the final judgment—the day when the eternal destiny of everyone will be determined—warning the crowd to believe the light while it shines before them.

✦ What Jesus does next might seem harsh, but we know that can't be true, since Jesus is never harsh. He was in the middle of teaching when his family came to see him—his mother and siblings. Whether he actually went out to say hello, we aren't told. But what do we learn from what Jesus says here about family?

....

....

....

....

7. WINDS AND WAVES (8:22-25)

Traveling efficiently from town to town in the region of Galilee often meant crossing the "lake" Jesus mentions in verse 22, which is actually the Sea of Galilee. During one such crossing, Jesus falls asleep in the boat. No doubt he was frequently tired, and perhaps the water was calm when they started out, lulling him to sleep. Soon after, however, a storm kicks up. The location of the sea makes it susceptible to sudden and violent storms when the east wind blows over the waters.[10] Even so, Jesus sleeps.

Joy Note

Jesus warns people to beware of the difference between deep joy in walking with him and joy that is superficial (Luke 8:13). *Real joy comes from the Holy Spirit and can be present in our hearts even when our plans and hopes don't go the way we want.*

✦ Why do you think Jesus is so calm while the disciples are panicked?

....

....

....

....

✦ What does Jesus say to the disciples about their reaction to the storm?

....

....

....

....

8. A LONELY MAN (8:26-39)

On the outskirts of the Gerasenes region, close to the shore, is a dismal and desolate place, the tombs, where the townspeople bury their dead. But the deceased aren't the only ones occupying this bleak place. A man lives there. The tombs are a fit dwelling for this man because in some ways he is dead even while he lives. Held under the oppressive power of demons, he wanders aimlessly, naked and alone. Luke tells us that Jesus's boat came on shore right near these tombs, and surely this is no coincidence.

Jesus has intended all along to encounter this tragic man and cast out the demons that possess him. This Jesus does, showing his authority once again even over the spirit realm.

✦ Skeptics today criticize the fact that Jesus killed a herd of pigs in the process of delivering the man, but they miss that there was a purpose in what happened to the pigs. What do the herdsmen, the owners of the pigs, do after the pigs have drowned, and what happens as a result?

✦ What is different about the man after his deliverance, and in what ways does his life change?

9. DAUGHTERS (8:40-56)

A prominent religious leader and a socially ostracized woman—Luke weaves their stories together here for a reason. The prominent man, Jairus, who heads up the local synagogue, comes to Jesus because his beloved daughter is dangerously ill. The woman, whose name we don't know, is contending with her own long-standing illness.

✦ What is different and what is the same about how Jairus and the woman each approach Jesus with their need?

· Differences:

· Similarities:

The public figure receives his miracle in private, while the social outcast is healed in public. One reason is that the woman's malady had left her socially unacceptable ("unclean" in Jewish law) and therefore isolated. She'd been virtually alone for twelve long years. By healing her publicly, everyone would know that she was ready to be welcomed back into society. So Jesus provides for her both physically and relationally.

✦ This is the only time in the Gospels that Jesus calls anyone "daughter." As you reflect on these two stories woven into one, what takeaway do you get from the references to daughters here?

By now, it's clear that Jesus is well known in the region. He's told several people to keep the miracles private, but news of his acts has spread anyway, and his powerful teaching has attracted ever-increasing crowds. The good news of the gospel is reaching people of all kinds, from the highest official to the lowest beggar.

LET'S TALK

1. No doubt shocking some, Jesus redefined family in 8:19–21. Of course, he loves and values family and calls us to cherish our relatives. At the same time, his remarks here show us how we are to prioritize our relationships. How has your commitment to Christ changed how you define family and relate to family members—both spiritual and biological?

2. The demon-possessed man at the tombs was a completely different person after Jesus healed him. He got his life back, we might say. Sin does to us what demons did to the man—holds us in bondage—until God frees us by uniting us to Jesus by faith. Discuss how you've changed through your relationship with Christ and how belonging to him has actually made you more *you*.

WHO *IS* THIS JESUS?

LUKE 9:1-50

Who exactly *is* Jesus? The crowds in Galilee want to know, and they speculate. Immoral leaders like Herod wonder too, and even Jesus's inner circle of twelve disciples isn't completely sure. Until now, Luke has been revealing Jesus Christ a little at a time, but this week we get a much fuller picture of who he is. We see it not only in the miracles Jesus does but also in his personal conversations and, of course, in his teaching. And as we understand more about who he is, we discover much more of what it means to follow him by faith. Concerning this week's study, it's worth pointing out here that the lesson is shorter than others, which might provide you with some leftover prep time to get a head start on Week 6, the longest lesson in our study.

1. MEN ON A MISSION (9:1-9)

We remember that Jesus has already singled out twelve men from among his many disciples and named them as apostles (6:12–16). Now the time has come to send them out on their first mission. Jesus limits their traveling supplies to just the basics; he wants them to travel light, so they can come and go easily from place to place.

✦ For what purpose were they sent out, and how did Jesus equip them for the task?

✦ What were the apostles told to do about those who refused to hear their message? In what way would this rather harsh gesture serve as a warning?

....

....

....

....

2. CURIOUS HEROD (9:7-9)

Like everyone in the region, Herod, the regional government official, has heard about Jesus—the miracles and crowds of followers. This Herod's name is Antipas, and he is the son of Herod the Great, the one who'd sought to kill the baby Jesus years earlier. The Herod here, Herod Antipas, is curious about Jesus.

✦ What three rumors has Herod heard about the identity of Jesus?

....

....

....

....

✦ What sad fact does Luke slip into this section?

....

....

....

....

3. A MIRACULOUS MEAL (9:10-17)

The apostles return from their mission, and they accompany Jesus to Bethsaida, the hometown of brothers Peter and Andrew and also of Philip. As always, crowds follow, hungry for hope and healing. On the outskirts of town Jesus ministers all day, but as evening draws near, practical considerations take over. Where will all these people find shelter for the night—and of even greater concern—what will they eat?

✦ The twelve urge Jesus to send the crowd into town for the night, but Jesus has another plan. How does Jesus set them up, in 9:13, for the miracle he is going to do?

✦ What does this miraculous provision of bread reveal about the nature of Jesus?

4. WHAT SAY YOU? (9:18-22)

When Luke shows Jesus praying, it's usually because something important is about to happen, and that is the case here. It unfolds in a conversation between Jesus and his inner circle. Jesus is going to ask them some questions. Of course, Jesus already knows the answers. His questions are just his way of getting his friends to think. So he draws them out, and then he gets to his main point: "Who do you say that I am?" Peter is the first to answer, and he identifies Jesus as "the Christ of God" (9:20). *Christ* is another word for Messiah. Peter recognizes that Jesus is the long-awaited Savior and King promised by God centuries before.

The twelve are beginning to grasp who Jesus is, but Jesus wants to keep his identity hidden from the public for the time being. As we know, God's people have been waiting for the promised Messiah, but they've been expecting a conquering military hero, someone to liberate them from the oppressive Roman authorities who make their lives difficult. But that's not what the actual Messiah—Jesus—has come to do.

✦ Most people reject God when he fails to meet their personal expectations. How is this shown in what Jesus reveals about himself in 9:22?

_____

_____

_____

_____

_____

_____

_____

Jesus Prays

- Before the disciples hear God's voice from heaven (3:21)
- Before selecting the twelve (6:12)
- Before asking the disciples their understanding of his identity (9:18)
- As God's glory is revealed to the disciples on the mountain (9:28-29)
- As he prepares to teach his disciples to pray (11:1)
- Before the devil is allowed to sift the disciples (22:32)
- Before he is arrested and taken away to be crucified (22:41-44)

5. SAVING YOUR LIFE (9:23-27)

Jesus has debunked wrong expectations about the Messiah and given his disciples a big dose of the real Christ. And with this fresh in their minds, he spells out the reality of what it means to belong to him.

✦ What three criteria for discipleship does Jesus give in 9:23?

1. _____

2. _____

3. _____

✦ Jesus gives a paradox—what seems like a contradiction—in verse 24, which he builds on in verses 25–26. What promise is given here and also what warning?

_____

_____

Jesus finishes this serious conversation in 9:27 with a special promise for three of his disciples—Peter, James, and John—who will live to see an amazing sight just eight days later.

> *"God has not given us our lives to keep for*
> *ourselves, but to give away for him."*[11]

6. GLORY ON THE MOUNTAIN (9:28–36)

Jesus prays again, this time high on a mountain with Peter, James, and John. As we've noticed, Jesus often prays when something really important is about to happen. This time, the important thing unfolds right during his prayer.

✦ The disciples have been sleeping while Jesus prays, but they begin to stir. Describe what they see as they wake up.

Jesus's three friends don't quite know what to make of this heavenly vision. They see Moses and Elijah talking with Jesus. We aren't told how they knew the identity of those two ancient men, but the fact that Moses and Elijah were recognizable indicates that we retain our unique identity after we die and that a day will come when we fellowship with the Lord and each other in heaven. As the disciples watch this miracle, the radiance of God's glory emanates from Jesus and reflects onto Moses and Elijah, but God keeps the disciples' gaze fixed directly on Jesus: "This is my Son, my Chosen One; listen to him!" (9:35).

Fast Facts about Moses and Elijah	
Moses (Exodus–Deuteronomy)	**Elijah (1 Kings 17–18)**
• Most important Old Testament prophet • Led God's people out of slavery in Egypt • Led God's people through the wilderness to the promised land • Witnessed a miraculous glimpse of God's glory • Received God's law on Mount Sinai and gave it to God's people	• A well-regarded prophet in Israel • Defeated God's enemies at Mount Carmel • Met with God on Mount Sinai • Performed miracles • Never experienced death

So why were Moses and Elijah even there? Well, Moses had been the primary Old Testament law giver, and Elijah had been the primary prophet, and their presence with Jesus here is meant to show the disciples that as great as those two Old Testament men had been, Jesus is greater in every way.

✤ As you reflect on all that's happened to the disciples in this chapter—activities and conversations—why do you think this amazing experience was such a vital blessing for them?

7. SLOW TO BELIEVE (9:37–43)

The very next day we find Jesus once again at the center of a large crowd. An anguished voice rises above all the conversational hum—a father pleading for the healing of his son who suffers seizures under the power of an unclean spirit. The boy's father had sought help from the disciples, but the disciples' attempts to expel the demon had failed. Only then does the desperate father turn directly to Jesus for help.

✦ Look back at Luke 9:1. How does that verse explain Jesus's holy frustration with the disciples here, especially in light of their experience on the mountain just one day earlier?

_____

_____

_____

The disciples have been slow to trust. Granted, they've had a lot to take in! But clearly Jesus doesn't see that as an excuse for unbelief. Perhaps that's why he begins his next revelation with a sharp command: "Let these words sink into your ears" (9:44).

✦ What does Jesus reveal here about his mission?

_____

_____

_____

Jesus is hinting at suffering yet to come—his death on the cross. The disciples don't get it. They look at each other with questioning faces, but none dares to speak up.

8. GROWING UP (9:46-50)

Grown-ups behaving like children—it happened in Jesus's day just as it does in ours, even among grown-ups who love the Lord. We see a bit of that here with the disciples at the end of this week's lesson.

✦ What are the disciples arguing about in 9:46?

_____

_____

_____

✦ Jesus uses a child to make a point to the arguing disciples. What is his point?

✦ The disciples are also disgruntled that someone outside their circle is doing miracle work. What does Jesus teach them—and us too—about how to evaluate and respond to those whose ministries aren't exactly like ours?

LET'S TALK

1. Consider the three aspects of genuine discipleship Jesus outlines in 9:23: "If anyone would come after me, let him deny himself and take up his cross daily and follow me." What does that entail for you at this present time?

2. Jesus asked his disciples to explain their understanding of who he is. How would you answer his question; in other words, who do *you* say that he is? It's easy to give the "right" answer—the one we're supposed to give. But what's really in your heart? Try to identify any areas of unbelief.

JOURNEY WITH JESUS

LUKE 9:51–19:27

How wonderful it would be if we could take our time studying every verse of Luke's Gospel, but with twenty-four chapters to cover in ten weeks, we simply can't. That's why we're covering a huge portion of the Gospel this week. Even so, it's a unified portion because we walk with Jesus from the beginning of his journey to Jerusalem almost all the way to the gates of the city. His journey begins with determination: "When the days drew near for him to be taken up, he set his face to go to Jerusalem" (9:51). In other words, it's the beginning of the end of Jesus's life on earth. When it is finished, Jesus will be taken back up to heaven. From the moment he begins this journey until he arrives in Jerusalem, we travel with him and see what his followers saw and what they learned along the way.

1. COUNT THE COST (9:51–10:24)

Miracles and healings have made Jesus popular, but as the full picture of his mission gets clearer, he experiences increasing rejection. We see it right here at the beginning of his journey, when he's turned away from a Samaritan village. Jesus and the disciples continue on their way, and as they journey along the road, they encounter three people who express a desire to come along with them.

Jesus Travels to Jerusalem[12]

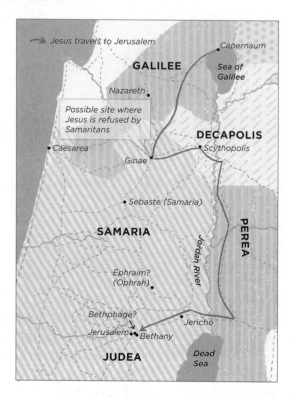

🕊 The first man they encounter offers to follow Jesus anywhere. What does Jesus's response in 9:58 reveal about the man's offer?

....

....

....

....

🕊 The second man they encounter wants to follow Jesus, but first he wants to see to the details of his father's funeral. Jesus's response might seem harsh, so it helps us to understand a bit more of what's going on here. The man isn't talking about attending the sort of funeral we have today. Back then, rites for the deceased and the burial process could take up to a full year. Even so, we've already seen that Jesus values family, and God expressly commands us to honor our parents. So here's where we apply a basic Bible study principle: *Let Scripture interpret Scripture.* Because the Bible is clear that honor is due to parents, we can know for sure that Jesus isn't telling this man that his family doesn't matter. So, with that in mind, why do you think he refuses this man's request to bury his father?

Bible study principle: Let Scripture interpret Scripture.

✦ The third would-be disciple offers to follow Jesus, but he wants to delay just a bit because of family concerns. His request seems reasonable, but Jesus tells him, "No one who puts his hand to the plow and looks back is fit for the kingdom of God" (9:62). Given the metaphor Jesus uses, it's likely he was speaking here to a farmer. What does Jesus's response to the man reveal about the man's heart for discipleship?

Before continuing on his journey, Jesus sends pairs of disciples—seventy-two in all—on ahead to various villages to prepare the townspeople for his coming (10:1–12). These disciples are to go house to house with the good news of the gospel. Even so, Jesus knows much rejection awaits him, and he warns the disciples to expect it as well, and he grieves over those who will refuse him. Some time later, the disciples return from what was in many ways a successful mission, and Jesus rejoices that God has opened the spiritual eyes of his disciples and humbled people to see the truth.

✤ What does Jesus reveal about himself and about God the Father in 10:22?

Joy Note

The disciples are joyful because their ministry efforts have been visibly successful, but Jesus cautions them to rejoice instead that their eternal destiny is secure (Luke 10:17–20). *While it's good to find joy in serving the Lord, our well-being isn't in what we do for him but in who we are in him.*

2. BEWARE (10:25–11:54)

Living for Jesus—that's the focus of this next leg of the journey to Jerusalem. Jesus and his followers encounter a lawyer as they travel. The lawyer wants eternal life, and he tries to paint himself as someone worthy to receive it, but Jesus opens his eyes with the parable of the good Samaritan to see that it's available only to those who know their desperate need of mercy.

Afterward Jesus comes to the home of two sisters, Mary and Martha, who become some of his closest friends. While he visits, he teaches them that fellowship with him matters more than doing things for him (10:38–42). Then on another occasion, a disciple asks Jesus for prayer help. "Teach us to pray," he says (11:1).

✤ In response to the disciple's request for guidance with prayer, Jesus gives them, in 11:2–4, what's called the "Lord's Prayer." What five petitions, or requests, are included in the prayer?

1.

2.

3.

4. ....

5. ....

✦ Jesus continues his prayer lesson with an illustration in 11:5–8 about helping a friend in need. What point is Jesus making about prayer here, and what does he go on to promise in verses 9–10 to those who pray as he instructs?

....

....

....

....

✦ What is promised in 11:11–13 to those who pray in faith?

....

....

....

....

As the journey continues, they encounter some people who accuse Jesus of being aligned with the devil, but Jesus silences them with the reality that God, not the devil, empowers his ministry. And then he warns his listeners, illustrating with a haunted house, that cleaning up our act—forsaking bad habits and going to church and doing good deeds—doesn't secure our salvation. Not just our words and our deeds, but first and foremost our hearts, must be given over to Jesus. Only then will we truly keep God's word (11:14–28).

The crowd is growing as Jesus speaks, so he teaches them more about himself. He is greater than the great Old Testament prophet Jonah and wiser than the famously wise King Solomon. He also teaches them more about discipleship, likening spiritual health to a well-lit lamp (11:29–36).

As he concludes his sermon, a Pharisee invites Jesus to his home for dinner, and Jesus accepts the invitation and accompanies the Pharisee to his house. Once there, however, things don't go smoothly. Jesus loves people so much that he never plays it safe with social niceties and pleasant mealtime conversation. After all, souls are at stake. Here, Jesus has no qualms about speaking the truth to his dinner companions, outing them as fools, pointing out their hypocrisy, and making dire predictions about their destiny.

✦ For what does Jesus foretell woe for the lawyers (also called "scribes") and the Pharisees in the following verses:

11:42 ....

11:43 ....

11:52 ....

Mixed in with those woes are other woes that don't make sense apart from a bit of Old Testament background. In 11:44 Jesus likens the Pharisees to "unmarked graves." According to Old Testament law, anyone who came in contact with a dead body—or even a gravesite—would become "unclean" as a result. Complicating matters was the very real possibility that someone would walk over an unmarked grave, becoming unclean in the process but being totally unaware of it. In the same way, people who followed the self-righteous teaching of the Pharisees became spiritually unclean but didn't even know it. That's why Jesus likens the Pharisees to "unmarked graves" here. He is condemning them for leading people astray. Another woe, the one in 11:47–51, is all about hypocrisy. These religious leaders made a big show of building flashy tombs for the prophets of old, even though, just like their ancestors, they despised those prophets for speaking the truth about God.

The dinner party stirred up hatred toward Jesus among the religious leaders, and they began to plot against him.

3. ARE YOU READY? (12:1–59)

Taking the long view—it's a challenge, isn't it? Many of us tend to be shortsighted because we're so used to fast solutions to our problems and provisions for our needs. But Jesus shows us that God's way is different. Some answers to prayer and deliverances and provisions come much later than we'd like, and some won't come at all until the next life. But one thing we can be sure of: sooner or later, guilty secrets will be revealed and all wrongs will be righted. And in the meantime, if we should suffer for our faith—yes, even die for it—we have no reason to fear because God takes careful note of every detail of every life. That's what taking the long view is all about. So when something we hope for is delayed, will we turn for comfort to what we can get out of this world, or will we wait for the Lord to act? Taking the long view is possible only if we trust in God.

✦ What reasons does Jesus give in 12:24–28 for why anxiety about our physical needs is pointless?

....

....

....

....

✦ God will always provide what we need until he calls us home to heaven; in other words, we will always have exactly what we need to carry out the particular callings God has for us at every point during our lives. According to 12:31–33, how is this reality meant to shape our focus?

....

....

....

....

✦ How have you experienced the truth of Jesus's words in 12:34?

....

....

....

....

Taking the long view means thinking past today and even tomorrow. In his parable of the wedding feast (12:35–40), Jesus calls us to hold onto an eternal perspective. We don't know when Jesus will return. What if it were today? Would we be glad, or would we be ashamed or afraid? We need to fix our eyes beyond our current circumstances. And this will help us when following Jesus proves costly, not only materially but in our relationships as well.

4. BE WARNED! (13:1-14:34)

Many are willing to embrace an inclusive, compassionate, and loving Jesus but not one who requires repentance from sin and obedience to God's word and ways. But there's no entrance into God's kingdom apart from real faith, which includes confessing sin and being willing to forsake it. That's included in the fruit Jesus mentions in his parable here about the barren fig tree. And Jesus tells two more parables in this section about God's kingdom, describing how it grows. Practical expressions of compassion and love are other indicators of genuine faith, as Jesus makes clear when he sharply rebukes a loveless religious leader.

✦ As Jesus and his followers continue toward Jerusalem, his teaching about God's kingdom prompts someone to ask him about the numbers. Will many be saved or just a few (13:23)? And Jesus's response redirects us instead to think simply about whether *we* will be saved. As you reflect on what Jesus has taught so far in Luke 13, why do you think he says that the door of entry is narrow?

Soon after this, Jesus is warned that Herod intends to kill him, but Jesus isn't bothered by Herod. Jesus knows he will continue to teach and heal until the time comes to fulfill his mission by dying on the cross in Jerusalem. Until then, Herod can't touch him. And as Jesus thinks about Jerusalem, his heart breaks for this special city, home of God's people and God's dwelling place for centuries. *If only . . .* , Jesus cries. If only they would come to him for mercy, they would find peace and protection. But they were not willing, and it breaks his heart (13:31–35).

Then at the beginning of Luke 14, once again we find Jesus dining with a group of Pharisees. He knows their hearts, that they've invited him in order to trap him and ruin his reputation, yet he eats with them anyway, and he silences them by miraculously healing one of the dinner guests. Then he tells them parables while they dine, teaching them about humility and genuine hospitality, no doubt inflaming their hatred even more.

✦ As they journey, the crowds grow larger. Jesus knows that many are following not because they really care about being with him, but because they want him to fix the broken places of their lives. So in 14:26–27 he clarifies what it takes to be a true disciple, and he brings in family again here, as he has done before when having similar discussions. Given what we've learned so far from Jesus's teaching overall, how are we meant to interpret his teaching in 14:26?

✦ Jesus uses a building contractor and a military leader to illustrate the nature of true discipleship. According to 14:33, what are true disciples willing to do if necessary?

5. LOST SHEEP, A LOST COIN, AND WAYWARD SONS (15:1–16:31)

By now it's become clear to us that Jesus attracts all sorts of people. And as word of his kindness spreads, even the sin-shamed and guilt-ridden dare to approach. As the Pharisees mock Jesus for associating with socially unacceptable types, Jesus responds to them as he so often does—with parables. This section of Luke's Gospel includes parables about a lost sheep (15:4–7), a lost coin (15:8–10), and a lost son (15:11–32).

✦ The parable about the lost son is really about two brothers, the younger of which is drawn to the pleasures he thinks he'll enjoy if he leaves home, but his adventure doesn't work out very well. Soon the younger brother realizes how good he'd had it back home, so he strategizes a plan for returning to his father. What sort of welcome does the son receive?

....

....

....

....

✦ Why is the older brother angry?

....

....

....

....

✦ As you consider the father's reaction to both sons, what does this teach us about God the Father?

....

....

....

....

....

....

....

Joy Note

Jesus reveals that all of heaven rejoices when one sinner on earth repents (Luke 15:7, 10). *We are able to please God by the choices we make.*

Jesus tells another parable in this section (16:1–13) about a dishonest business manager, and his point here is that worldly unbelievers sometimes show more skill in stewarding their money than believers do. Jesus is in no way promoting dishonesty; he just wants his followers to be smart about their personal resources. The Pharisees took special note of this particular parable because they loved anything to do with money, but they reject the kingdom Jesus is opening before them (16:14–17). They don't want grace and mercy—they want to earn heaven by keeping Old Testament laws. They don't realize that they simply can't do it. For all they brag about keeping the law, they break it left and right, like when it comes to divorce, which Jesus points out here. Finally, Jesus concludes this section with a scary parable about hearing him and responding before it's too late. He is the only way into God's kingdom (16:19–31).

6. HOW DISCIPLES LIVE (17:1-37)

Conversing with his disciples once again, Jesus warns about safeguarding people against sin but also readily forgiving them when they do. Hearing these high standards, the disciples ask for more faith, but Jesus tells them that greater faith isn't the answer—it's leaning on the one in whom their faith rests. And going the distance in the Christian life requires humility—recognizing that Jesus owes us nothing but that we owe him everything—and such recognition breeds joy and gratitude.

Beginning with John the Baptist right up until now, when Jesus journeys to Jerusalem, the kingdom of God has been unfolding right in front of the crowds. Jesus has actually brought the kingdom by coming to earth as a man. Even so, the Pharisees have missed it, so Jesus tells them again: "The kingdom of God is in the midst of you" (17:21).

✦ The kingdom has already come—yet not fully. It will continue to unfold, first at the cross, and then fully later on, when Jesus returns to earth at some future time. According to Jesus, what will his return be like?

....

....

....

....

✝ Jesus conveys a sense of urgency about his eventual return and along with it a warning to remember Lot's wife (17:32), a woman who wasn't committed to the Lord wholeheartedly. (You can read her story in Genesis 19:1–26.) As you ponder what Jesus is saying in this section, how do you understand his words in 17:33: "Whoever seeks to preserve his life will lose it, but whoever loses his life will keep it"?

....

....

....

....

7. FROM EVERY WALK OF LIFE (18:1–43)

Jesus tells two more parables on the journey. The first is meant to encourage God's people to pray for relief from suffering and injustice because God cares for them and will deliver them in his perfect way and time (18:1–8). The second parable compares an arrogant attitude of self-righteousness with a tender heart of humility, which is a necessity for receiving God's grace and mercy (18:9–14). The needy dependence of children illustrates Jesus's lesson on humility. As children rely on adults to care for their every need, so must followers of Jesus depend on him.

A successful young man had been listening to Jesus, and he is drawn by what he hears. "Good Teacher," he asks, "what must I do to inherit eternal life?" (18:18). Jesus calls out the young man on his use of the word *good*. He wants the man to see two things. First, Jesus wants the young man to think carefully about calling Jesus "Good Teacher." Since only God is truly good, the young man should apply that word to Jesus only if he believes that Jesus is actually God. Second, Jesus wants the young man to see that obedience to God's law doesn't count if it's not done from the heart. In all this, Jesus is probing the young man's heart. It's what Jesus does with everyone, and he knows exactly how to do it with each and every individual. In the case here, it involves the young man's money.

✝ How does Jesus expose the young man's heart? See 18:22–23.

....

....

....

....

✤ As you consider this encounter (18:18–30), why do you think that wealth can be such a hindrance to embracing Jesus that only God is able to overcome it?

....

....

....

....

✤ What does Jesus promise to those who value him above everything else?

....

....

....

....

Jesus and the disciples are drawing nearer to Jerusalem, so he details for the twelve the suffering that awaits him, but they aren't yet ready to take it all in (18:31–34). As they approach the ancient city of Jericho, a blind beggar along the road cries out for mercy. Jesus knows that the man wants his vision restored, but he compels him to express this desire clearly so the crowd will see what happens, and then he restores the man's sight (18:35–43).

8. REDEEMING THE TIME (19:1–27)

Jesus's reputation has spread through Jericho even before he enters this ancient city. A tax collector named Zacchaeus is among the crowd, hoping for a glimpse of Jesus, but Zacchaeus has a couple of problems. First, he's a short man, so he can't see over the people in front of him. Plus, as the head tax collector in Jericho, he'd become quite rich taking money from people. Surely no one is eager to step aside so Zacchaeus can get a better look. But Zacchaeus is determined, so he climbs a tree to watch Jesus pass by. Then the all-knowing, compassionate Jesus gives dignity to the undignified tax collector by inviting himself to dine in Zacchaeus's home, and Zacchaeus in turn gives his life to Jesus (19:1–10).

Afterward, because Jesus is now so close to Jerusalem, he tells one more parable about God's kingdom (19:11–27). He wants to stamp on his listeners' minds that the kingdom he's opening up is not about a military takeover. And we can understand the kingdom a bit more clearly as we identify the characters in the parable. The nobleman, of course, is Jesus himself; the servants are those who set out to serve him; and the citizens are those who reject his message.

✤ What does this parable reveal about the way we steward our talents and resources?

....

....

....

....

✤ What does the unfruitful servant reveal about how unbelief affects our view of God?

....

....

....

....

....

....

....

Joy Note

The lost and lonely Zacchaeus is filled with joy when Jesus invites himself over for dinner (Luke 19:6). *Countless blessings, both in this lifetime and later in heaven, come to us when we welcome Jesus into our lives.*

The parable does *not* teach that failing to fully use our gifts will cause us to lose our place in God's kingdom. Rather, it indicates that if we do nothing for God, likely we never had faith in the first place. In other words, fruitfulness doesn't earn salvation; it simply demonstrates that we have it.

So ends the journey. Jesus and his disciples are poised to enter Jerusalem, where Jesus will spend the next week—the last week of his earthly life.

LET'S TALK

1. Review the incident that took place in the home of Mary and Martha (10:38–42). Where do you see yourself in the story—are you more naturally like Mary or Martha? What practical application can you get from this incident and apply personally?

....

....

....

....

....

....

2. Jesus revealed what really held the heart of the rich young man—his wealth (18:18–23). The man said that he wanted to follow Jesus—he even believed he really wanted to—until Jesus exposed his true priority. How might the Holy Spirit be speaking to your heart through this story? Is there something that competes with Jesus for first place in your heart? The way to know is your willingness to give it up.

....

....

....

....

....

....

....

3. Which of Jesus's teachings on his journey to Jerusalem most challenges you or grips your heart? Consider his teaching on prayer, on the cost of following him, on trusting him and not worrying, or on the priority of love and compassion.

....

....

....

....

....

....

....

....

THE BEGINNING OF THE END

LUKE 19:28-21:38

The journey is over. Jesus has arrived at the city of Jerusalem, the centuries-old home of God's people. The heart of the city is the great Jewish temple where the people come to celebrate special occasions like the Feast of Passover or the dedication of a firstborn son. But it won't always be that way. In fact, Jerusalem's days are numbered. As for God's people whose roots are in this city, the Jews, will they embrace Jesus as the Messiah, the King of kings? Or will they reject him? Their eternal destiny depends on how they answer. But that's just as true today as it was back then. We all must decide—will we acknowledge Jesus as our Lord and Savior? It's a life-or-death decision.

1. O, JERUSALEM! (19:28-48)

Jesus pauses outside Jerusalem to prepare to enter the city gates. As we'll see, the details of his entry prove that he's the long-awaited Messiah.

✦ Read the prophecy found in Zechariah 9:9. How, in Luke 19:29–35, do we see Jesus fulfilling that prophecy?

As Jesus rides, the disciples spread out their cloaks on the road. It's how royalty was greeted in those days. (Other Gospels mention the waving of leafy palm branches, which is why we commemorate this day as "Palm Sunday.") As they advance to the city, large numbers come and add their garments to the roadway and offer praises to God. This is the only hour of Jesus's earthly life that he is publicly acknowledged as King of kings. The Pharisees, jealous of the attention Jesus is receiving, try to stop the adulation, but they cannot.

✧ When the city comes into full view, Jesus weeps for what will happen to those who refuse to see and hear his message. According to Jesus in 19:43–44, what will happen to Jerusalem in years to come?

✧ Jesus goes home, so to speak, to the temple, the house of God. Throughout the Old Testament right up to the time of Jesus, the temple was where God's people enjoyed God's presence. That was about to change because Jesus, through his death, was going to open a new, better way into God's presence. At this point, however, the temple is still central, and Jesus is angry when he enters because the religious leaders are making people—even poor people—pay money to worship God. As you consider all we've learned about Jesus, why do you think he is so angry here?

2. ASKED AND ANSWERED (20:1-26)

After ridding the temple of harmful people, Jesus returns daily to preach the good news of God's kingdom, and many are mesmerized by him. This makes the temple leaders so jealous that they fantasize about how to destroy Jesus, but because he's so

Jerusalem at the Time of Jesus[13]

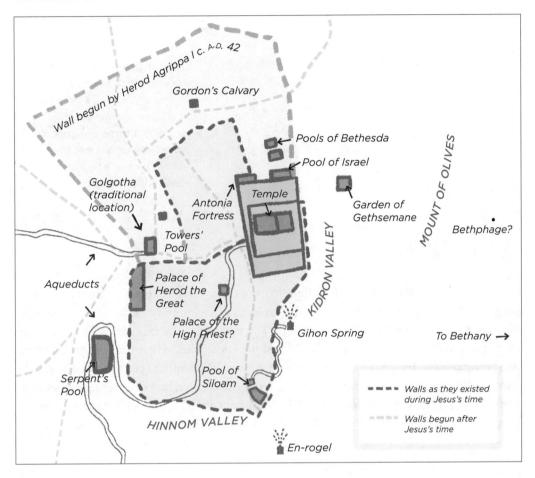

Wall begun by Herod Agrippa I c. A.D. 42

Gordon's Calvary

Pools of Bethesda

Pool of Israel

MOUNT OF OLIVES

Golgotha (traditional location)

Antonia Fortress

Temple

Garden of Gethsemane

Bethphage?

Towers' Pool

KIDRON VALLEY

Aqueducts

Palace of Herod the Great

Palace of the High Priest?

Gihon Spring

To Bethany →

Serpent's Pool

Pool of Siloam

Walls as they existed during Jesus's time

Walls begun after Jesus's time

HINNOM VALLEY

En-rogel

popular, they don't dare. Instead, they question his authority to teach and preach. But Jesus turns the tables on them, asking them to share their knowledge of the now deceased John the Baptist. The temple leaders don't really care about John or anything else to do with the true Messiah, so they try to come with an answer that will simply make them look like the religious superiors they crave to be. It backfires, proving once again that Jesus is wiser and more powerful.

✠ As Jesus goes about Jerusalem, in and out of the temple, many people love him, but even more hate him. So he tells a parable about a vineyard owner who was despised by his tenants (20:9–16). Why did the tenants hate the owner and harm those he sent?

Cornerstone
The cornerstone of a building is designed to fit into a corner or angle of a building. It is often engraved with a prominent name or a special date and then set into the wall as part of a building dedication ceremony.

Given the unpleasant outcome for the tenants in the parable, those in the crowd who suspect it's really about them brush off what Jesus is saying here. So Jesus reinforces his message straight from the Old Testament: "The stone that the builders rejected has become the cornerstone" (Psalm 118:22). As best we know, back when the first great temple was being built in the days of King Solomon, a beautiful stone carved specifically for the temple wall was rejected because it was the wrong size. Later, however, it turned out to be a perfect fit for the cornerstone—the most important stone in any building. Jesus reveals here that he is the stone of Psalm 118, and all who reject him will be rejected by God.

✦ The religious leaders—the scribes and Pharisees—are no dummies. They're well aware that Jesus is directing his warnings to them, so they continue to look for ways to get rid of him. Their next scheme involves questioning Jesus on the hot-button issue of Roman taxes. They think they've finally got him, but he silences them with a coin. What principle does Jesus teach us in how he answers in 20:25?

3. HYPOCRISY EXPOSED (20:27-47)

Next to question Jesus are the Sadducees, a Jewish sect that didn't believe in the after-life. Because Jesus's teaching threatens their beliefs, they too want to harm him.

✦ The Sadducees try to confound Jesus with an outlandish scenario about a fictional widow and her seven husbands, but once again, he leaves the tricksters speechless with his answer. What do we learn from Jesus here about the afterlife?

Jesus reinforces the reality of the afterlife by quoting from the Old Testament. He has in mind the time when Moses refers to the Lord as "the God of Abraham and the God of Isaac and the God of Jacob" (20:37). Those patriarchs—Abraham, Isaac, and Jacob—were long dead by Moses's day, but God is still their God. And then he humbles the pride of the religious leaders by provoking them to fail an oral exam on Psalm 110. Jesus isn't playing games with the leaders here in 20:41–44. He's trying to show them—and the gathered crowd—who he really is. Yes, he's the promised "son" of David, but he is just as much David's Lord, as David wrote in Psalm 110.

✦ Jesus turns to his disciples and, in front of everyone, he exposes the vile behavior of the scribes in particular. For what does Jesus condemn them in 20:45–47?

4. KEEP WATCH! (21:1-38)

Jesus is about to wrap up his time in the temple, and as we'll see, he finishes on a somber note as he reveals what's going to happen in Jerusalem in the years ahead and, on a much larger scale, what will happen to the whole world one day.

✦ Jesus not only teaches in the temple; he does a lot of observing, and one thing he sees in his line of vision is the offering box. What do we learn from Jesus's assessment of the givers he sees in 21:1–4?

Jesus also does a lot of listening in the temple, and he overhears a conversation about all the riches, the precious metals and gemstones, that are part of the temple structure. After listening, Jesus reveals that all this grandeur will one day be gone. Quite naturally, the disciples want to know when and how this will happen. "When will these things be," they ask, "and what will be the sign when these things are about to take place?" (21:7).

Jesus answers their question about the temple's destruction, but his answer actually covers not just one but two future events. The first event will be local, right there in Jerusalem. In about forty years' time, the Romans would sweep in and destroy the temple and kill the majority of Jews living in the city. The second event is what happens to the whole world when Jesus returns at the end of time. Jesus's primary focus here is on the first event, but his words are meant to point beyond that to the much greater fulfillment of his second coming and the final judgment.

> *"Studying Luke 21 is a little bit like wearing bifocals.*
> *The destruction of the temple is near at hand. . . .*
> *Yet the end of the world is always in the background,*
> *and we constantly need to keep it in our gaze."*[14]

✦ How in 21:8–9 does Jesus answer his disciples' question in 21:7 about timing?

Jesus describes in 21:10–12 the awful things that will happen leading up to the destruction in Jerusalem. These same things—wars and famines and pestilences—have been occurring worldwide ever since, and they are a warning of the final judgment to come.

To prepare his disciples for the destruction of Jerusalem, Jesus tells his disciples to remain faithful when the Romans come for them, even if they are killed in the process. And he warns that all believers should flee the city when the armies begin to invade. No matter what happens, Jesus says, their eternal destiny is secure. When the destruction began some forty years later, those who'd trusted his words did flee, and countless Christians survived as a result. But those who'd scorned his warnings all perished.

✤ Jesus moves on to the bigger, final event—the end of the world. According to 21:25–26, what signs will precede his return?

✤ How will Jesus return to earth?

✤ We don't know the particulars about when Jesus will return, but he does make clear how his followers are to live while they wait for him. As we watch and wait, what three things in 21:34 are we instructed to guard against?

1.

2.

3.

LET'S TALK

1. Jesus warns against the attitude of the scribes in 20:45–47. In what circumstances might you be tempted to put on a show of looking and acting religious, hiding the fact that you don't have your spiritual act completely pulled together? What underlies the temptation, and what steps can you take to overcome it?

2. Jesus never answers the question about when he will return to take us home to heaven forever, but he does instruct us how to live in the meantime: "Stay awake at all times" (21:36). He certainly didn't mean we should avoid sleep! He was talking about being mindful of his return. Have you been "sleeping" your way through some aspects of your Christian life? Here are some examples of how we "sleep":

· Avoidance rather than trust
· Delay obedience to something we know God wants us to do
· Hoard our resources of time and money and love

If you've been "sleeping," identify some practical ways you can wake yourself up.

THE POWER OF DARKNESS

LUKE 22:1-71

The time has come for Jesus to finish his earthly mission. First, though, he will share a final meal with the twelve. Afterward he will be arrested, tried, and found guilty— all within twenty-four hours. He knows that he's going to suffer physical abuse, but most painful will be the heartbreak of betrayal, rejection, and abandonment. As Jesus prepares for the end, he moves about Jerusalem accepting the things that must unfold according to God's plan.

1. BETRAYED (22:1-6)

We know very little about Judas, one of the twelve—until now, when Satan enters into him. He has never been a true disciple.

✦ What does Judas do after Satan enters into him?

....

....

....

....

✦ What clue are we given in 22:5 about what really holds Judas's heart?

....

....

2. FEASTING WITH JESUS (22:7-23)

Jerusalem is crowded with people who have traveled to the city for the annual Passover celebration, a holiday that commemorates Israel's miraculous deliverance from Egypt (you can get details about this holiday in Exodus 12:1–14). Jesus has arranged to enjoy the meal with his disciples on Thursday evening, plans that will keep him hidden from his enemies until the feast is over.

✦ How does Jesus instruct Peter and John to prepare in 22:7–13?

✦ Jesus has anticipated this time with the twelve because it will be his last meal with them in this lifetime. They share a cup of thanksgiving, and then Jesus breaks a loaf of bread before their eyes. What does he tell them in 22:19 as he passes the bread?

"It was the last supper in a number of ways: the last meal that Jesus would eat with his disciples, the last meal that Jesus would eat in his pre-glorified body, and the final Passover meal of the old covenant."[15]

Timeline of Jesus's Last Week	
Sunday	Jesus enters Jerusalem.
Monday	Jesus rids the temple of profiteers.
Tuesday	Jesus teaches in the temple.
Wednesday	Jesus teaches in the temple.
Thursday	Jesus eats the Last Supper with the twelve and then prays in the garden of Gethsemane.
Friday	Jesus is arrested, tried, convicted, and executed and then laid in a tomb.
Saturday	Jesus's disciples rest for the Sabbath.
Sunday	Jesus is raised back to life and appears to his friends.

✦ After they'd finished eating, Jesus passes another cup of wine. What does he tell them in 22:20 about this cup?

With the bread and wine, Jesus is revealing what's about to happen to him and what will happen when his work is done. God's people will no longer live under the Old

Testament law of Moses, the requirement of endless bloody animal sacrifices to atone for their sins. In place of those sacrifices, Jesus is about to sacrifice himself, which will free people from ever having to atone for sin again. To this day, Christians follow his command to eat the bread and drink the cup as a reminder of what he's done for us. We call it "the Lord's Supper" or "Communion."

✤ What does Jesus reveal in 20:21–22, and how do the disciples react in 20:23?

....

....

....

....

3. AFTER-DINNER CONVERSATIONS (22:24–38)

Déjà vu. The dinner conversation has escalated into an argument, and it's one we've heard before (back in 9:46). The disciples are debating which of them will wind up with A-list spiritual-celebrity status.

✤ Jesus intervenes in the argument, promising them that in the age to come, they will indeed receive special honor. In the meantime, however, that's not the point. How does Jesus explain true greatness?

....

....

....

....

Then Jesus turns directly to Peter and warns, "Satan demanded to have you, that he might sift you like wheat" (22:31). The "you" in this verse is plural, which means that Satan intends the downfall of all the disciples, not just Peter. Even so, what Jesus says next, in 22:32, is directed just to Peter.

✤ How does Jesus deal with Satan's demand, and what will be the outcome?

....

....

✤ How does Peter's response here in 22:33 link back to the conversation in 22:24–27 about which one is greatest?

During the meal, Jesus has revealed to the disciples what is about to happen to him, and he has also given them a glimpse of what will happen to them. Finally, he prepares them for the work they'll do after he's gone. Their missionary endeavors will require them to be good stewards of their personal resources.

4. ON THE MOUNT OF OLIVES (22:39-53)

Most likely for safety reasons, and for privacy, Jesus has been spending nights on the outskirts of the city, just to the east, on the Mount of Olives. That's where we find him now along with the disciples.

✤ After instructing the disciples how to pray, Jesus wanders a short distance to pray by himself. As he prepares to face the darkest hour of his life, what does Jesus ask his heavenly Father, and how is he answered?

No doubt Jesus feels lonely when he returns to the disciples and finds them sleeping. But he doesn't focus on himself. He's concerned for their welfare, so he reiterates the importance of prayer. As he is speaking, a hate-filled mob approaches (22:45–47).

✦ What tone does Jesus take toward Judas as he confronts Judas's callous betrayal?

....

....

....

....

✦ How does Jesus respond to the mob who has come to arrest him?

· To the servant of the high priest:

....

....

....

· To his disciples:

....

....

....

· To the chief priests and officers:

....

....

....

5. AT THE HOUSE OF THE HIGH PRIEST (22:54–65)

Jesus is taken from the garden and led forcefully to the house of Caiaphas, the Jewish high priest, even though it's nighttime. The disciples had fled when Jesus was arrested, but Peter follows the mob at a safe distance and then manages to gain entry into Caiaphas's courtyard, where a fire is burning. The warmth of the fire's light on that dark night draws Peter, and he joins those gathered around it.

✤ What happens to Peter in the hours leading up to dawn, and how does he handle it?

✤ Meanwhile, Jesus is abused by his captors and mocked for daring to be identified as the Messiah. What clue do we get in 22:65 that Jesus is who he claims to be—the Son of God?

6. SHAM TRIAL (22:66–71)

As the Friday morning sun rises in the sky, Jesus is forced to appear before the entire Jewish council. This religious body, called "the Sanhedrin," is made up of men—seventy elders and the high priest—who generally hate Jesus.

✤ The religious leaders have been biding their time, waiting to get rid of Jesus. For three years he has disrupted their way of life and sidelined the power they hold over God's people. So, of course, they twist every word Jesus says against him. That's why, when they demand, "If you are the Christ, tell us" (22:67), he refuses to give them a direct answer. He knows they've already made up their minds about him, and they won't believe, no matter what he says. Even so, what does he reveal about his identity?

LET'S TALK

1. As we reflect on what Jesus said about Satan's desire to sift the disciples (22:31–32), we can better understand how the power of evil works in our own lives. Satan desires to destroy each one of us, but he can do nothing without God's permission. How can this truth help you manage anxiety and conquer besetting sins?

....

....

....

....

....

....

....

2. The disciples never quite got past their craving for greatness. But are we really much different? As you consider what Jesus told them—a true leader is one who serves (22:26–27)—can you detect where your own thinking in this regard might be skewed? Identify ministry leaders you admire and the ministry they do, and consider what attracts you to them and the way they serve.

....

....

....

....

....

....

....

CRUCIFY HIM!

LUKE 23:1-56

Morning has dawned on the last day of Jesus's earthly life. The Jewish authorities, the Sanhedrin, have imprisoned him on a trumped-up charge of blasphemy, which, according to Old Testament law, deserves the death penalty. And that's exactly what these leaders demand because they hate Jesus so much. So Jesus is dragged from one place to another, suffering mockery and physical abuse, until they get their way. But all those murderous participants don't yet know that God is the one controlling these events and overseeing every detail for the good of his people.

1. JESUS TRIED AND CONVICTED (23:1-25)

The Sanhedrin convict Jesus on the charge of blasphemy. To blaspheme is to belittle the name of God or treat him with contempt, and the Jewish penalty for blasphemers was death. The Sanhedrin cannot actually carry out the death sentence because all the Jewish people—including the leaders—are under the rule of Rome. If they want to execute Jesus, they have to get the go-ahead from Roman officials. So they force Jesus into the presence of a Roman governor named Pontius Pilate, who happens to be in Jerusalem to control the crowds during the chaotic week of Passover.

✦ Pilate, like other Roman officials, couldn't care less about Jewish religious rules. The Sanhedrin know this, of course, so they need to find a way to make Jesus seem guilty of civil offenses rather than religious ones. How do they attempt this in 23:1–5?

....

....

....

....

As Pilate examines Jesus, he is perplexed. The gentle man before him, badly beaten, hardly looks like a criminal trying to stage a coup against Rome. But Pilate is well aware of the hatred toward Jesus and what the mob wants him to do, so he finds himself in a fix. That's the trouble with being a people-pleaser like Pilate. But he's presented with a way out of his dilemma when he discovers Jesus's hometown is in Galilee. Pilate can get out from under the need to deal with Jesus by sending him to a Galilean official—Herod.

✦ How does Herod react when he first sees Jesus?

....

....

....

....

✦ Why and how does Herod's initial reaction to Jesus change?

....

....

....

....

✦ What to do with Jesus? It becomes Pilate's problem once again. In an attempt to appease the people, what solution does Pilate propose in 23:16?

....

....

....

....

✦ How is the matter finally resolved?

....

....

....

....

> *"What will we do with Jesus? As we see Jesus go through these trials in Luke's Gospel, we need to reach a verdict about him in our own minds and hearts. Will we declare his saving innocence or will we try to push him away as Pilate did?"*[16]

2. CRUCIFIED! (23:26-43)

Condemned! Jesus has been sentenced to die by crucifixion, a horrible punishment designed to inflict maximum pain and humiliation. As part of the sentence, the condemned were flogged before being nailed to the cross, and after the flogging, they were made to carry their own cross, weighing close to 40 pounds, to the place of execution. Weakened from the flogging and staggering under the weight of the cross, Jesus struggles with every step, so a man named Simon, just going about his business, is forced to carry the heavy cross for him.

✦ Along the way Jesus finds strength to give his final prophecy, once again foretelling the coming destruction of Jerusalem and the people in it. Those who reject him—the green, healthy wood—will burn up quickly like dry branches. How does Jesus redirect the weeping women in 23:28, and what does this indicate about his focus as he struggles?

....

....

....

....

✦ What is the focus of Jesus's prayer in 23:34 as he is being crucified?

....

....

....

....

✦ Customarily, the particular crime for which the condemned was being crucified was written on a sign and hung around his neck or inscribed over the cross so that passersby would know the reason for the execution and be warned not to break the law themselves. What is inscribed over Jesus's cross?

....

....

....

....

✦ What differences do you see in 23:39–43 between the two criminals crucified on either side of Jesus?

....

....

....

....

3. DEATH OF JESUS (23:44-49)

Jesus, the Son of God, has been nailed to a cross by the power of evil, so it's fitting that at the brightest hour of the day—noon—darkness creeps over the sun and covers the land until three o'clock. The darkness is a sign of God's judgment against sin, falling fully on his Son for sins he never committed. Like the silence that signals an approaching storm, the sudden noonday darkness surely hushes the chaotic crowd.

What happens in the temple is even more shocking: the heavy curtain, 60 feet high, which blocked people from entering the Most Holy Place, miraculously rips apart from top to bottom. The Most Holy Place was so sacred that only the high priest had ever been inside, and even he was allowed in only one day a year. On that day, the Day of Atonement, he was required to bring animal sacrifices to pay for the sins of God's people, and in this way, people maintained their fellowship with God. This had been the system ever since the days of Moses centuries before. But now this sacred room is wide open!

✦ What does the ripped curtain reveal about Jesus and the death he died? You might want to glance at Hebrews 9:11–15 to help you answer.

✦ Even the smallest details happening this day prove that Jesus is who he's claimed to be—the Messiah, the Son of God—because even these details were foretold centuries earlier. How are these passages from Psalms fulfilled here at the cross?

   • Psalm 22:7–8

   • Psalm 22:16–18

· Psalm 31:5

✦ How do the people observing the crucifixion respond to the miraculous happenings at Jesus's death?

· The centurion:

· The crowds:

· His acquaintances and followers:

4. JESUS'S BURIAL (23:50–56)

Not every member of the Sanhedrin is a Jesus hater. One man, Joseph of Arimathea, risks his reputation and perhaps even his well-being by asking permission to take Jesus's lifeless body off the cross for burial. We aren't told much about Joseph, but we know he's wealthy since he owns his own burial tomb. And whether by riches or reputation or both, he has sufficient clout to get in to see Pilate and make his request.

Pilate gives the okay, so Joseph returns to the cross and carefully removes the body of Jesus. It's the day of Preparation for the Sabbath, so Joseph works efficiently to finish the burial by sundown, when the Sabbath begins. Once it starts, Joseph will have to refrain from such physical labor of any kind until the Sabbath is over.

✦ Who else witnesses the burial of Jesus, and what do they do afterward?

....

....

....

....

Jesus has been laid in Joseph's tomb, and with the Sabbath beginning, the women have done all they can do until Sunday comes.

LET'S TALK

1. Two thieves were crucified alongside Jesus. One rejected him right up until death, but the other turned to him in faith and was saved. What do we learn from this incident about the nature of salvation? As you think about loved ones who don't know Jesus, how can this story encourage you to pray for them and tell them about the gift of salvation?

....

....

....

....

....

....

....

2. Like so many others, Pilate didn't want to deal with Jesus, so he pushed him away. Do you find yourself pushing Jesus away when following him proves costly? We might not renounce him outright, but sometimes we want to keep some part of our lives— a habit, a desire, a relationship—just for ourselves. Is there something like this in your life, and if so, what will you do with Jesus?

HE IS RISEN!

LUKE 24:1-53

Sunday has come, the first day of the week. The Sabbath is over, and people get back to the business of everyday life. But this isn't going to be an ordinary Sunday. Jerusalem is still packed with travelers for the Passover celebration, which, of course, has been overshadowed by the public execution of the popular Galilean preacher Jesus. For the past three years rumor has circulated throughout Galilee that Jesus is the long-awaited Messiah, but for many, his crucifixion kills that hope. Those who'd known him personally waken on Sunday with grief-filled hearts, unable to bear the loss of their teacher and friend—and, yes, their Lord. Bewilderment mixes with grief as they try to make sense of it all. But in just a matter of hours, their grief will turn to joy.

1. WHERE IS JESUS? (24:1-12)

The pale violet light of early dawn aids the women as they hurry back to the tomb on Sunday to anoint the body of Jesus with burial spices. As they draw near to the grave, they wonder if dim morning shadows are playing tricks on their eyes because the tomb appears wide open, its large stone covering pushed to one side. It's not an illusion! And Jesus is no longer inside.

✦ What do the two men—the angels—tell the women about Jesus?

....

....

....

....

✛ The astonished women rush back to tell Jesus's inner circle, now eleven, since Judas
  is gone. How do the men, including Peter, react to the news the women bring?

....

....

....

....

2. EMMAUS ROAD (24:13-35)

Later that Sunday, two other disciples leave Jerusalem on foot for a seven-mile walk to
the village of Emmaus. One is named Cleopas. We aren't told the name of his traveling companion. As the two walk and talk, a stranger suddenly appears alongside them.
"What is this conversation that you are holding with each other as you walk?" he asks
(24:17). They have no idea the stranger is actually Jesus as they recount for him the
events of the past three days—the unjust death of the miracle-working teacher, the
dashed hopes, and the perplexing disappearance of his body from the tomb.

> *"If Jesus happened to overtake you on the Emmaus*
> *Road, would you invite him to stay?"*[17]

✛ According to Jesus, in 24:25, what has hindered Cleopas and his friend from understanding all that's happened?

....

....

....

....

✤ What do we learn from Jesus in 24:25–27 about the Bible?

✤ As afternoon dims to evening, Cleopas and his friend arrive home. They are enjoy-
ing their conversation with this stranger so much that they urge him to come stay
awhile before he continues on his way. What opens their eyes to recognize Jesus,
and what do they do afterward?

Jesus has risen! That's the amazing news. He is not dead after all!

3. JESUS PREPARES TO LEAVE (24:36-53)

During this time, after Jesus's resurrection, he talks with people, and he mysteriously
comes and goes, just as he did with Cleopas and his friend on the road to Emmaus.
When he suddenly appears in the midst of the gathered disciples, they are understand-
ably scared at first because they think Jesus is a ghost.

✤ What do we learn in 24:39–43 about Jesus's resurrected body?

✤ How, according to 24:45, are the disciples enabled to understand the Bible?

....

....

....

....

....

....

....

Joy Note

The disciples are overcome with astonished joy when Jesus appears to them after he is raised from death (Luke 24:41). *Walking with Jesus leads to ever-richer discoveries about him that seem almost too good to be true.*

✤ We're told that the disciples "disbelieved for joy" (24:41) when they recognized Jesus in his resurrected body. Why do you think Luke describes the disciples' reaction that way?

....

....

....

....

✤ How does Jesus summarize the entire Bible in 24:44–47?

....

....

....

....

After opening the eyes of his disciples to understand the Bible, Jesus prepares them for the work they will do for the rest of their lives. Because they are eyewitnesses to his life and work and death, they are especially equipped to tell others who he is and what he came to do for God's people. He gives them practical instructions too, telling them to remain in Jerusalem until they are "clothed with power from on high" (24:49). This power that will clothe them is the promised Holy Spirit. (We find out all about this Spirit-given power in Luke's second volume, the book of Acts. For now, you might just take a minute to glance at Acts 2:1–4.)

✦ Finally, forty days after Jesus was raised from death, he leads his disciples outside the city to one of his favorite places on the Mount of Olives. While he is blessing his beloved friends, he is taken up to heaven. How has the disciples' outlook about Jesus changed during these forty days?

....

....

....

....

....

....

....

Joy Note

Joy. That's what Jesus brings to all who believe. That's why the angel who announced his birth proclaimed, "Fear not, for behold, I bring you good news of great joy that will be for all the people" (2:10). And it's why, at the very end, he leaves joy behind when he returns to the Father in heaven. Are you certain? That's why Luke wrote the story of Jesus, that you may know. May the truth of Jesus— Son of God, son of Man, prophet, priest, and King of kings—fill your heart with joy.

After Jesus returns to heaven, the disciples are filled with joy because everything promised about Jesus has turned out to be true (Luke 24:52). *If we trust in Jesus and follow the way he has marked out for us in his word, we will know personally the blessing of every promise he ever made.*

LET'S TALK

1. Jesus lingered on earth for forty days after he was raised from death because he wanted to be with people he loved and reveal himself to them. Still today he wants to be with people and reveal himself, which he does throughout his word, the Bible. Do you regularly sit with him and listen to what he says? Or has Bible reading become one more item on your daily to-do list? If your time in the word isn't all you'd like it to be, name some practical ways to change your approach.

2. As we come to the end of Luke's Gospel, note what you've learned or what's affected you most about:

· the person of Jesus:

· the way of salvation:

· the path of discipleship:

HELPFUL RESOURCES
ON LUKE

Ferguson, Sinclair. *To Seek and to Save: Daily Reflections on the Road to the Cross*. Surrey, UK: Good Book Company, 2020.

Köstenberger, Andreas J., and Justin Taylor. *The Final Days of Jesus: The Most Important Week of the Most Important Person Who Ever Lived*. Wheaton, IL: Crossway, 2014.

Köstenberger, Andreas J., and Justin Taylor. *The First Days of Jesus: The Story of the Incarnation*. Wheaton, IL: Crossway, 2015.

Ryken, Philip G. *Luke, Volume 1: Chapters 1–12*. Reformed Expository Commentary, ed. Philip G. Ryken and Richard D. Phillips. Phillipsburg, NJ: P&R, 2009.

Ryken, Philip G. *Luke, Volume 2: Chapters 13–24*, Reformed Expository Commentary, ed. Philip G. Ryken and Richard D. Phillips. Phillipsburg, NJ: P&R, 2009.

NOTES

1. Wayne Grudem and Thomas R. Schreiner, "Introduction to Luke," in ESV° Study Bible (Wheaton, IL: Crossway, 2008), 1938.
2. "The Setting of Luke" map from page 1937 of the ESV° Study Bible (The Holy Bible, English Standard Version°), copyright ©2008 by Crossway, a publishing ministry of Good News Publishers. Used by permission. All rights reserved.
3. Philip G. Ryken, *Luke, Volume 1: Chapters 1–12*, Reformed Expository Commentary, ed. Philip G. Ryken and Richard D. Phillips (Phillipsburg, NJ: P&R, 2009), n.p.
4. Ryken, *Luke, Volume 1*, 57.
5. "Jewish and Roman Rulers" chart from pages 1786–1787 of the ESV° Study Bible.
6. Ryken, *Luke, Volume 1*, 152.
7. "Jesus's Ministry in Galilee" map from page 1955 of the ESV° Study Bible.
8. If you want to dig into the biblical call to discern right from wrong, you might want to start with 1 Corinthians 5:11–13, Ephesians 5:6–10, and 1 John 4:1.
9. Ryken, *Luke, Volume 1*, 355.
10. Ray Vander Laan, "Sea of Galilee Geography," That the World May Know, accessed April 17, 2020, https://www.thattheworldmayknow.com/sea-of-galilee-geography.
11. Ryken, *Luke, Volume 1*, 462.
12. "Jesus Travels to Jerusalem" map from page 1996 of the ESV° Study Bible.
13. "Jerusalem at the Time of Jesus" map from page 1999 of the ESV° Study Bible.
14. Philip G. Ryken, *Luke, Volume 2: Chapters 13–24*, Reformed Expository Commentary, ed. Philip G. Ryken and Richard D. Phillips (Phillipsburg, NJ: P&R, 2009), 412.
15. Andreas J. Köstenberger and Justin Taylor, *The Final Days of Jesus: The Most Important Week of the Most Important Person Who Ever Lived* (Wheaton, IL: Crossway, 2014), 60.
16. Ryken, *Luke, Volume 2*, 559.
17. Ryken, *Luke, Volume 2*, 656.

Also Available in the
Flourish Bible Study Series

For more information, visit **crossway.org**.